The BUTCHER'S TABLE

Quarto.com

© 2023 Quarto Publishing Group USA Inc.
Text © 2023 Allison D'Andrea

First Published in 2023 by The Harvard Common Press, an imprint of The Quarto Group,
100 Cummings Center, Suite 265-D, Beverly, MA 01915, USA.
T (978) 282-9590 F (978) 283-2742

The Harvard Common Press titles are also available at discount for retail, wholesale, promotional, and bulk purchase. For details, contact the Special Sales Manager by email at specialsales@quarto.com or by mail at The Quarto Group, Attn: Special Sales Manager, 100 Cummings Center, Suite 265-D, Beverly, MA 01915, USA.

27 26 25 24 23   1 2 3 4 5

ISBN: 978-0-7603-8155-7

Digital edition published in 2023
eISBN: 978-0-7603-8156-4

Library of Congress Cataloging-in-Publication Data available.

Design and Page Layout: Tanya Jacobson, tanyajacobson.co
Cover Image: Zack Bowen, zack-bowen.com
Photography: Zack Bowen, zack-bowen.com, and Nick Berger (pages 6, 8, 161, 189)
Food Stylist: Catrine Kelty, www.ckfoodstylist.com
Illustration: Ada Grace Keesler and Shutterstock (pages 14 and 17)

Printed in China

The BUTCHER'S TABLE

TECHNIQUES AND RECIPES TO MAKE THE MOST OF YOUR MEAT

Allie D'Andrea

CREATOR OF OUTDOORS ALLIE

HARVARD COMMON PRESS

Contents

INTRODUCTION

*E*very cut of meat has its own blueprint, a set of qualities—the tenderness, fat content, flavor, size, and shape—that indicates how it can best be prepared. By learning how to butcher your own meat, you'll gain a deeper understanding of different cuts and their characteristics.

This book might change the way you think about each cut of meat, and it can certainly help you find your bearings while butchering at home. Use it as a guide to gain comfort in the kitchen, maximizing the potential of each unique cut of meat from chicken to pork and venison.

You can learn to butcher and master every cut of meat at home, no matter your experience level. I know because it happened to me.

I was twenty-one when I saw a deer harvested for the first time. I remember the drops of red on the snow that left a trail to where her body laid underneath an oak tree. Nick, my partner at the time and now my husband, dragged the doe by the legs to a flat spot and started the process of field dressing. I had a background in emergency medicine, but nothing prepares you for watching the guts of a deer being removed for the first time. Nick hung the cleaned carcass and worked to break it down into manageable pieces before wrapping it in freezer paper and labeling it with a marker.

Hunting was the catalyst of my desire to learn how to butcher. The knowledge I gained from processing my own wild game flowed into a desire to learn about all types of meat. I can thank my family for that.

***

Whether they realize it or not, my parents taught me that food brings people together. Every weeknight of my entire childhood, all six of us ate dinner as a family at the kitchen table in our customary "assigned" seats. My mom is a fabulous home cook: Chicken and broccoli, beef stew, and vegetable soup are a few of her classic dishes that we (my brothers, sister, and I) love and fondly remember from our family dinners growing up.

My dad's parents grew up in Italy and moved to America in the 1960s. They brought with them traditional methods of curing meat and pasta making. Their love of food was reflected in their luscious garden, homemade pasta sauce, and dry aged prosciutto. I have fond memories of being a kid eating pastina, salami, and fresh melon during every visit to their home.

My grandma's house, on the other hand, was more of the wild west with food (in the best way). I'd consider it a traditional American upbringing. We snacked on Sunny D and buttered toast, chicken nuggets and French fries, and frequently visited the candy store at the mall.

***

For someone who grew up on chicken, pork, and beef, eating venison felt foreign at first. Although it's no surprise that as my butchering and cooking skills improved, my love of eating venison did too.

I think that's why I made this book in a way that lets you choose your own adventure. If you are an avid hunter—like many of my followers and community— you can dive right into the venison chapter. You'll find everything you need to unlock the potential of wild harvested deer. On the other hand, if you are sourcing your meat and are more interested in breaking down, say, a half hog you bought from a local farm, then start with the pig section.

The chicken chapter is included for a couple reasons. First, I find chickens are a great gateway into butchery for those with no experience. They tend to be the least expensive and easiest to source. I also think that cooking your way through a few recipes in the chicken chapter can help you gain confidence in connecting why particular cuts of meat lend themselves to specific cooking techniques.

That said, many of the lessons in the chicken chapter can be applied to wild game birds.

The general anatomy and techniques used for chicken will supply you with everything you need to dress wild game birds of all kinds, from quail to pheasant, chukar to grouse. And if you choose to cook a chicken recipe with game birds, simply scale the recipe for the amount of meat you're cooking.

***

No matter where you want to start in this book, keep in mind this comforting thought: Even if you don't butcher something perfectly the first time, it's impossible to totally fail. Meat can always be cooked— just maybe in a different way. Take, for example, accidently cutting a fillet minion so badly that you don't have reasonably sized steaks to cook. Well, just keep going and cut it into cubes. It's no longer a steak, but you're about to have meat for one fabulous stew. If you remain flexible and creative, you will eat well as you learn!

Last but not least, I encourage you to read through the next few pages before you try any of my recipes. You'll find a few techniques, tips, and ingredient recommendations that are important to me and my style of cooking. I included them because I want every recipe you cook from this book to be one you enjoy—and hopefully one you are excited to share with family and friends.

Cheers,

CHAPTER

1

Welcome to My Kitchen

INGREDIENTS

Before we get into the specifics of butchery, knives, and the more unique content of this book, I want to cover the ingredients you'll find throughout. I believe that quality ingredients can elevate a particular cut of meat to its highest potential. Some of the items listed on the following pages are essential, and the outcome of your dish will suffer without them. Others are more of a suggestion and a personal preference that I've developed over time. Thus, these ingredients are listed in order from the most important to less important.

Salt. Kosher salt is the king of all salts. Derived exclusively from sodium chloride (no iodine, as in table salt), it gives you a lot of control over your food's seasoning. You can season, taste, season, taste, without as much of a risk of oversalting.

The large crystals are great for drawing out moisture from meat, which is why I use kosher salt when presalting meat 24 hours before cooking (see page 22). Think of kosher salt as a tool to enhance flavors, not just an additive to make food salty.

Diamond Crystal is my go-to brand, but what's important is to just choose a brand and use it consistently. Over time you'll learn how much will affect the level of salt in your food and become better at predicting how much is needed when seasoning a dish.

If you commit one thing to memory here, it's that 1 teaspoon (7.8 g) of kosher salt *does not equal* 1 teaspoon (6 g) of table salt.

All recipes in this book call for kosher salt.

Garlic. Whatever you do, avoid jarred, minced garlic. Instead, spend a few dollars on a garlic press and discover leveraging the robust flavors of fresh garlic.

When shopping for garlic, look for cloves that aren't too soft or too dry. They should be firm, without soft spots or sprouts. Occasionally, powdered garlic is called for in a recipe to create a smooth texture (see my chicken meatball recipe, page 72).

Herbs. "Fresh is best" holds true when it comes to herbs. Hardy, sturdy-stemmed herbs like rosemary and thyme should be added early in cooking, as they can withstand temperatures while imparting flavor throughout the cooking process.

Delicate, soft-stemmed herbs should be carefully chopped to prevent bruising and added toward the end of cooking, with just enough time to release their bright flavors.

Because dried herbs have a lower moisture content, their flavors are more concentrated. For that reason, add less dry herbs than you would fresh herbs. A good ratio is one to two. For example, 2 tablespoons (5 g) of fresh basil is about 1 tablespoon (2 g) of dried basil.

It's important to add dried herbs early so they have time to re-absorb moisture and flavor your dish.

Basic Herbs

- **Hard Stem:** Bay leaves, oregano, rosemary, sage, thyme
- **Soft Stem:** Basil, chives, cilantro/coriander, dill, parsley

Yogurt. Whether a recipe calls for regular plain yogurt or plain Greek yogurt, go for full fat (4 to 5 percent). Full-fat yogurts add a creamy texture and tangy flavor to marinades, sauces, and dips that you just can't achieve with nonfat options.

Extra virgin olive oil (EVOO). A daily staple for searing, sautéing, and marinating, EVOO has a smoke point of 375°F (190.5°C), which is not great for high-temperature cooking. Extra virgin olive oils provide rich flavor during the cooking process, though, and they're fabulous for vinaigrettes or dressing a dish. Spend as much as your budget will allow for a high-quality EVOO. Look for one sold in a dark bottle and use it for finishing dishes.

Avocado oil. I reach for avocado oil almost as often as olive oil. Avocado oil has a high smoke point, around 520°F (271°C), and a mild buttery flavor that works well for basically every recipe. I would never finish a dish with avocado oil, but for sautéing, searing, and grilling, I reach for the avocado oil.

Eggs. There's a stark difference in color between pasture-raised eggs and a cage-free eggs. Pasture-raised eggs have a strong yellow-orange yolk, rich in flavor, while cage-free eggs are cloudy and muted in color and flavor.

All of these terms (cage-free, free-range, pasture-raised) sound the same, but there is a major difference in the quality of the eggs based on their origin. Just remember: Only buy pasture-raised eggs. Everything else is subpar. Pasture-raised eggs are expensive, but they're worth it.

All recipes in this book call for large-size eggs.

Butter. To maintain full control over seasoning, always opt for unsalted butter. You're looking for butter that is creamy and rich with yellow color.

Kerrygold pure Irish butter contains a higher butterfat content than most butters available in the grocery store. And because the cows are grass fed, you'll notice the same intensity in color that we see in the yolk of pasture-raised eggs.

I opt for Kerrygold in most cases, but, ultimately, it's your job to taste your food, season, taste, and repeat until it's perfectly palatable. If you choose salted butter, the process is the same: Taste, season, and repeat until you're satisfied with the taste.

Black pepper. The flavor in black peppercorns dissipates quickly after grinding. Your pepper should be freshly ground to maintain as much spicy punch as possible. Purchase whole dried black peppercorns (which will stay good for up to a year in your pantry) and a quality grinder that is capable of delivering both a fine or a coarse grind.

KNIVES AND TOOLS FOR BUTCHERY

To become an efficient home butcher, you need the proper tools for the job. Butchering a pig without a boning knife is like trying to putt with a driver. Will it get the job done? Yes, but not efficiently. Do yourself a favor and make butchering at home easy with the following tools.

BONING KNIFE

The boning knife is your single most important tool as a home butcher. (I've processed plenty of whitetail deer with nothing more than a single boning knife.) As the name implies, a boning knife is used to remove the bones from the meat. These knives have a characteristic look, with a long, thin blade and a sharp, pointed tip that can easily reach tight spaces between meat and bones. Boning knife blades are offered in a few different styles, each intended for a specific use.

Here are some general comparisons of boning knife qualities and what to look for depending on the work you want to do.

Curved versus straight

Curved blades are for delicate jobs (think poultry and fowl) or working around the small spaces within a joint. Straight blades work well for thicker, tougher chunks of flesh, when you want precision and straight cuts while portioning. For breaking down larger animals like pig or deer, it's helpful to have both types of blades on hand.

Flexible versus stiff

Flexible blades provide nuanced cutting and allow the knife to cut around joints with ease, but what makes flexible blades great at one task makes them poor for others. Flexible blades can bend and go off course when slicing through thicker meats. Stiff blades, on the other hand, are designed for thicker meats and do well with broad, straight cuts. Looking for something in the middle? A semi-flex blade provides the best of both worlds, providing enough bend to work around a bone without too much wandering when trying to make a straight cut.

Boning knife versus fillet knife

It's easy to confuse a boning knife with a fillet knife. After all, they are similar in size and blade shape, and there are even some boning blades that are designed to serve both purposes. A fillet knife is specifically designed to separate fish meat from bones and skin. Due to the delicate nature of fish meat, a fillet knife is thin, usually curved, and extremely sharp; it's perfectly designed for precision. A knife like this typically ranges from 4 to 9 inches (10 to 23 cm) in length and is very flexible. Don't use a fillet knife to bone meat: its light, flexible blades lack the ability to cut through thick meat and can lead to injury. Boning knives are stiffer and thicker than fillet knives, offering the toughness needed to easily cut through meat.

BUTCHER KNIFE

CIMETER

CLEAVER

BONING KNIFE

BREAKING KNIFE

The breaking knife offers force and strength for slicing larger cuts of meat or even breaking through small bones or joints. It typically ranges from 8 to 10 inches (20 to 25 cm) in length, with a strong and sturdy curved blade. This type of knife is heavy and excels at breaking down larger pieces of meat into smaller cuts, allowing for smooth cutting no matter how tough the meat.

CIMETER

The cimeter's large blade allows for clean, flat cuts through meat without creating sawing marks. Think of the cimeter as the last knife in the butchering process. It typically ranges from 10 to 12 inches (25 to 30 cm) in length and is a go-to knife for creating a clean presentation while steaking, removing pork skin, and trimming. A cimeter is lighter than a breaking knife, yet sturdier and larger than a boning knife. You'd reach for a cimeter after the animal has been broken down to create clean, crisp secondary cuts like chops and steaks.

BUTCHER KNIFE

The butcher knife boasts a large, straight, sturdy blade with a curved tip. It is a versatile option whose function dances somewhere between a breaking knife and a cimeter, as it can be used to break down large cuts of meat into smaller cuts of meat, perform various trimming tasks, and cleanly slice steaks without saw marks.

Note: Sometimes you'll see the term "butcher knife" used as a catchall term to describe breaking knives, cimeters, and other long-bladed, sturdy knives used for breaking down meat.

BONE SAW

The bone saw is designed for sawing through bones. They have large, wide, and deep teeth that can cut through bone without clogging up, as can often happen with saws that have fine, shallow teeth. Bone saws range from 1 to 2 feet (30 to 60 cm) in length and are an essential item to have when butchering pork or venison.

OTHER CUTTING TOOLS

Slicing Knife

The slicing knife is thin and long, ideal for slicing prosciutto or other cured ham. The blade is typically 10 inches (25 cm) in length and straight with a rounded tip. Some also feature Granton edges, which helps to slice meat thin without tearing it.

Cleaver and Mallet

The meat cleaver is one of the most iconic butcher knives, with its broad, hefty blade. Meat cleavers are designed to chop through soft bones, like ribs, and joints with ease. They're one of the heaviest knives in the kitchen and perform best when properly used with a rubber mallet. Bone saws are often used in place of cleavers in our time, but the nostalgia of breaking through bones with a traditional piece of equipment like a meat cleaver has its appeal.

Poultry Shears

Poultry shears are kitchen scissors specially designed for butchering poultry. They have a different shape than traditional kitchen shears and are ideal for cutting through poultry bones and meat safely.

OTHER BUTCHERING TOOLS

Butcher's Twine

This special grade of twine is a must-have for trussing poultry and tying off roasts. Sometimes called kitchen or cooking twine, butcher's twine is made of 100 percent cotton and offered in various ply ratings. It is designed to withstand the high heat of an oven or smoker, but it shouldn't be exposed to an open flame.

Bench Scraper

Bench scrapers are important for keeping your work area clean. Throughout the butchering process, animal fat, flesh, and gunk will build up and create a slimy workspace. A metal bench scraper that is easy to sanitize will help keep things clean.

Bone Dust Scraper

After sawing through bone, you are left with a dusty mess of bone and meat particles that can coat the surface of the meat (especially when using a band saw on bone-in cuts). Instead of scraping this unpalatable paste off with your knife and dulling the edge, use a bone dust scraper to scrape away debris after sawing.

Meat Hook

Meat hooks are like an extension of your hand, with a sharp precision tip that allows for easier pulling and handling of meat during the butchering process. They're a handy tool to have for removing the membrane on ribs, keeping your non-knife hand out of harm's way, and cleaning bones while frenching.

SHOPPING FOR AND MAINTAINING KNIVES AND TOOLS

HANDLE MATERIALS

A wide range of options are available for handle materials for knives and other kitchen tools. It's important to consider comfort, affordability, and other factors like maintenance and aesthetics when choosing a handle material.

MATERIAL	PROS	CONS
Wood	Traditional style	Not as durable
	Attractive look	Can trap bacteria
	Comfortable to use	Expensive
	Provides excellent balance	Requires maintenance
	Nonslip	
Composite	Made of resin and wood or other natural materials	Not as well balanced
		Not as durable
	Attractive look	
	Affordable	
	Nonslip	
Plastic	Affordable	Not as comfortable
	Easy to clean	Not as attractive
	Low maintenance	
	Nonslip	
Stainless steel	Easy to clean	Not as comfortable
	Durable	Slippery when wet
	Low maintenance	

BLADE MATERIALS

A sharp blade with good edge retention is important for butchering. Look for high-carbon stainless steel, which is a quality material known for holding its sharpness over time. This goes for poultry shear blades and bone saw blades as well.

Tang

The blade on some knives runs continuously from the point of the blade to the butt of the handle. This is referred to as full tang, which creates a well-balanced, durable knife. A sub tang, or half tang, knife will be more affordable, but it will not offer the same durability or balance.

KNIFE SHARPENING

A dull knife is a dangerous knife. More force is required when cutting with a dull blade. This can lead to slips and accidents. A dull knife doesn't slice through the meat; it rips through it and therefore lacks precision. Put simply, there is no reason *not* to keep your blade razor sharp.

Honing Rod

It's counterintuitive, but keeping a knife sharp has more to do with frequent honing than with sharpening. Most often, the blade has microserrations that need to be realigned, and honing is the way to do it. Sharpening, on the other hand, removes metal from the blade and should only be done when honing doesn't produce a sharp edge. Polished steel honing rods won't remove material from your knife's edge and are your best option to for regular use. For minor upkeep that goes a step further, you can use a coarse-grit honing rod occasionally to keep your knife's edge for a longer time before you need to sharpen it.

Sharpening

When your knife's edge is dull and cannot be brought back to life with a honing rod, it's time to use a sharpening tool. Sharpening stones remove the least amount of blade material and create an excellent edge, but they require a bit of knowledge to be used properly. Electric sharpeners are extremely easy to use, but they usually remove a lot of blade material. If sharpened too frequently, your knife could lose its balance and become unusable. If sharpening at home isn't for you, send your knives to a professional: it's well worth the cost.

MEAT PREPARATION

THAW MEAT THE RIGHT WAY

You forgot to pull the chicken breast out of the freezer and you're scrambling to defrost it in time for dinner. You decide to cheat and turn to the microwave. Three minutes later, you're left with a partially cooked, tough chicken breast.

It happens to the best of us, but there are better options when it comes to thawing meat—and not all of them take twenty-four hours.

Refrigerator method. The refrigerator method is the best method for defrosting frozen meat. Take your meat out of the freezer and put it directly into the refrigerator for twenty-four hours until it is completely thawed. Larger cuts of meat, like whole chicken or pork butt, will take longer, up to forty-eight hours to thaw in the refrigerator. This method is gentle on the meat and creates the best end product.

Thaw plate method. Thaw plates are affordable and easy to use. Typically made of aluminum, an excellent heat conductor, a thaw plate's tray conducts the ambient room temperature to defrost frozen meat faster than if it sat on the counter. Place a sealed bag of frozen meat on the thaw plate and allow three to four hours for it to defrost, flipping once to ensure even thawing.

Cold water method. This might be the quickest hack for thawing meat safely and efficiently. Completely submerge a sealed bag of frozen meat in a bowl of cold tap water. Allow it to thaw for one to two hours until completely defrosted. The larger the cut of meat, the longer it will take to thaw.

Note: Avoid the spread of bacteria and skip rinsing your meat. The risk of spreading contaminants is higher when meat is rinsed because the water can splash from the meat onto the counter, all over the sink, and onto other unwanted places. Always wash your hands, your sink, and all prep areas thoroughly before and after cooking.

SALTING, MARINATING, AND BRINING: THE HOLY TRINITY OF FLAVOR AND MOISTURE

Salting. Salting meat in advance improves the flavor and tenderness of any cut of meat. The salt draws moisture from the area of greatest concentration (the inside of the meat) to the area of least concentration (the surface of the meat) through a process called osmosis. With a bit of time that moisture mixes with the salt, essentially creating a brine, which moves back into the meat along with the seasoning of the salt. This process causes the meat to hold on to the moisture better, even after cooking.

> **Tip:** I like to salt meat twenty-four hours prior to cooking to give the salt time to work its magic. I apply an even coating of kosher salt to all sides of the meat and place it in the refrigerator until I'm ready to cook. I always salt my meat in advance, unless I plan on marinating or brining it instead.

ESSENTIAL · ESSENTIAL ·

Marinating. A marinade adds flavor with the aid of oil, herbs, spices, and glutamate-rich ingredients like soy sauce. Most herbs and spices are soluble in oil: they release their full flavors when mixed in oil, which then penetrates the meat's surface. Without salt—or salty ingredients like soy sauce—the flavors will only penetrate the outer layer of the meat. That's why I always add salt to my marinades to maximize their effectiveness. Salt also helps increase moisture, so a good marinade enhance flavors *and* juiciness in your meat.

Brining. A brine is a solution of salt and water, sometimes with sugar and herbs or spices, which moistens and tenderizes while also getting the flavor deep into the meat. Similar to salting, this process moves from the area of greatest concentration (the liquid brine) to the area of least concentration (the meat), infusing the meat with flavor through osmosis. During this process, the salt changes the structure of the proteins within the fibers of the meat, allowing it to retain moisture even after cooking. That liquid contains flavors from the herbs, sugars, and spices in the brine, which seasons the meat all the way through instead of just on the surface, as with a marinade. It also tenderizes the meat by breaking down the structural integrity of its proteins, creating a more enjoyable eating experience.

Brining is an essential tool for lean meat, like venison, and moistening meat that frequently dries out, like pork and chicken. You'll have a harder time getting a brown, crispy sear on the outside of the meat with brining, but often the tradeoff is worth it.

TIPS FOR EVEN COOKING

Uneven cooking is one of the challenges of cooking a whole chicken. While a portion of the meat will be cooked to juicy perfection, the remaining bits will either be undercooked or unpalatably dry.

There are a few reasons for uneven cooking, but we have ways to solve them.

Temperature prior to cooking. If you take a venison steak directly from the refrigerator and slap it onto a hot pan, the result is an overcooked outer rim with an underdone center. Or, if you take a whole chicken from the cold fridge and place it in a hot oven, the lean breast meat will reach doneness much faster than the dark thigh meat tucked deeply around the hips.

The solution is to allow the meat to come to near room temperature before cooking it. I like to rest meat on the kitchen counter for thirty minutes to an hour before cooking: this allows the meat's internal temperature to gently rise in an even fashion and gives the best chance for even cooking.

Uniform shape. Take a fatty, boneless blade roast from a pig and you'll notice it's not uniform in its shape. A chicken breast suffers from the same problem: It's thick on one side and thin on the other. When cuts of meat aren't evenly shaped, they can be overcooked in some spots and undercooked in others.

Tying roasts with kitchen twine combats this issue by squeezing all of the meat into a condensed, uniform shape that stays put through the cooking process. This helps the meat cook evenly, and the twine can be removed before serving.

Mallet. Pounding the meat with a mallet can create an even cut of meat, especially when preparing steaks or chicken breast. Place the cut of meat in a plastic bag and use a heavy object like a meat mallet or rolling pin to pound down the thick portions until the entire cut of meat is the same thickness throughout.

Butcher's knot. The butcher's knot is a useful way to secure large cuts of meat in a uniform shape, creating a beautiful presentation and assisting in even cooking. A style of slipknot, it's easily tightened and is commonly tied with butcher's twine. I opt for butcher's twine that is made of 100 percent cotton, as it's both food and oven safe.

On the following page, you'll find instructions for using a butcher's knot to tie up a roast.

HOW TO TIE A BUTCHER'S KNOT

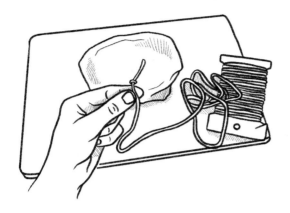

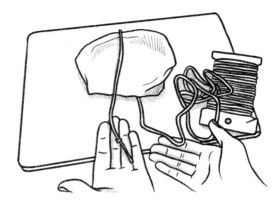

1. Tie an overhand knot in the free end of the string.

2. Slide the twine under the roast and fold the knotted string back toward you over the top of the roast. The knotted string should be on the left, with the long string on the right.

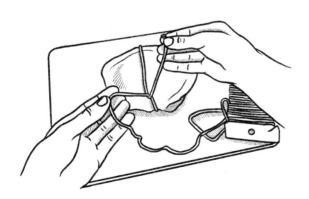

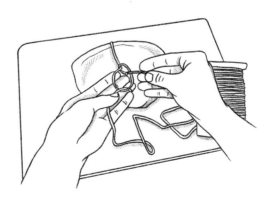

3. Pull the knotted end toward you, then around the long string.

4. Make a loop around the long string with the knotted string and pull the knotted string through the loop.

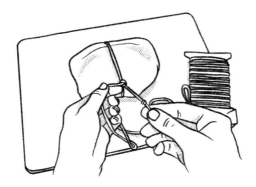

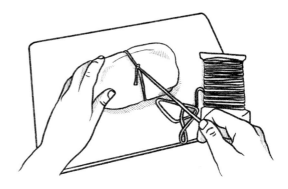

5. Pull the knotted string toward you until a second knot forms.

6. Pull the long string toward you, then away from you and repeat back and forth until the two knots come together and the twine is snug against the roast.

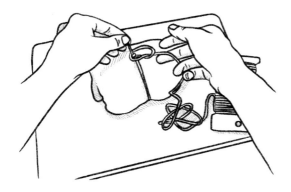

7. Take the long string and make a loop around the knots.

8. Pull the long string to tighten and trim the excess. Repeat every 2 inches (5 cm).

PERFECT SEAR

Drying the outside of a cut of meat with paper towels before searing helps create the brown crispy crust we want. Without drying, any moisture on the outside of the meat will begin to steam as soon as the meat hits the pan. Steaming instead of searing ruins the desired brown crust, and we're left with a limp, colorless, flavorless "crust."

You can't get a good sear if you don't have a hot pan. Preheat the pan over medium-high heat for two minutes, then add oil and give it another minute or two to heat up. You'll know the oil is ready to go when it moves like water as you tilt the pan and it just barely begins to smoke.

If a flavorful browned sear is what you're after, it's important to avoid overcrowding the pan. When there's too much meat packed in a pan, the moisture can't escape, which leads to steaming. The solution is simple: Sear your meat in small batches.

After the meat is added to the pan, press it down with your hand or a spatula to ensure that it touches the surface of the pan evenly. After that, don't touch the meat until you're ready to flip it. Moving, poking, or prying the meat as it sears will only cause heat to escape and interferes with the browning process. Resist the urge to touch.

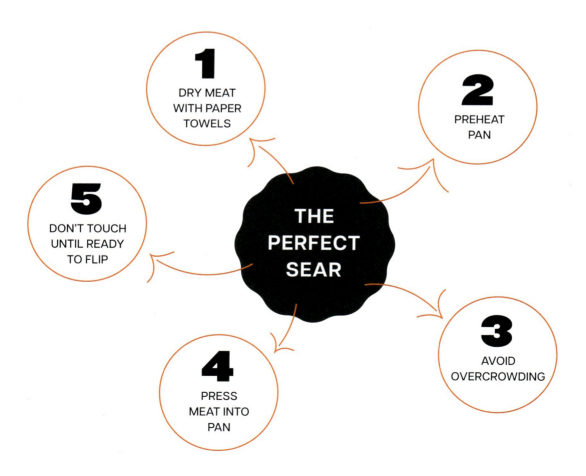

1 DRY MEAT WITH PAPER TOWELS

2 PREHEAT PAN

THE PERFECT SEAR

3 AVOID OVERCROWDING

4 PRESS MEAT INTO PAN

5 DON'T TOUCH UNTIL READY TO FLIP

RESTING MEAT

Resting meat after cooking is critical for preserving its juiciness. We rest meat to redistribute the juices throughout the meat, a process that locks in moisture and flavor instead of allowing it to spill onto the cutting board. A thin steak should rest for about ten minutes after cooking, while a thick roast should rest anywhere from fifteen to twenty minutes.

INTERNAL TEMPERATURE

Overcooking meat leads to dreadfully dry, tough meat. The best way to avoid this problem is to closely monitor the internal temperature of the meat as it cooks. A simple meat thermometer is inexpensive and fits in even a crowded kitchen drawer. The tip of the thermometer should be inserted into the thickest part of the meat for the most accurate reading. I recommend cooking tender venison steaks to medium rare, which is an internal temperature 130°F (54°C); this will keep the meat juicy and flavorful. Pork and poultry require higher internal temperatures to be considered safe to eat: Pork must be cooked to 145°F (63°C); poultry, 165°F (74°C).

The exception to this rule comes when you're cooking low and slow, like slow roasting, braising, or barbecuing. Tough cuts of meat will remain seized up until higher internal temperatures are reached, at which point the meat will relax and become fork tender. This occurs somewhere between 165°F to 200°F (74°C to 93°C), depending on the cut and recipe.

DRY HEAT VERSUS MOIST HEAT

The method of cooking you choose to prepare a cut of meat should always be selected based on the tenderness or toughness of your meat. For example, the bottom round of a deer is a tough cut that, if pan-fried, will cause your jaw to ache from chewing through each bite.

Tender cuts of meat, like venison tenderloin, pork chops, or chicken breasts, can be cooked in dry- or moist-heat methods. Extremely tough cuts, on the other hand, like venison shanks, must be cooked longer in lower temperatures by moist-heat methods in order to soften the strong connective tissues and break down the tough meat into palatable bites. Some cuts of meat are somewhere between tender and tough, so they can handle lower-temperature dry-heat methods as long as the cut has been brined or marinated first.

METHOD	DRY VS MOIST	TENDER VS TOUGH	DESCRIPTION
Roasting	Dry heat	Tender cuts of meat can be roasted 300°F to 375°F (150°C to 191°C). Tougher cuts of meat should be slow roasted at temperatures of 300°F (150°C) or lower.	Meat is cooked by heated air circulating around it, usually in the oven.
Grilling/barbecuing	Dry heat	Tender cuts of meat can be grilled at high temperatures over direct flames. Tougher cuts of meat should be cooked slowly in a cooler zone of the grill to cook them through gently.	Meat is cooked by a flame heating a metal grill, sometimes with smoke from wood chips to add flavor.
Braising	Moist heat	This is my favorite method to transform large, extremely tough cuts of meat into something fall-apart delicious. I do not recommend this method for tender cuts of meat.	Meat is first browned at a high temperature, then simmered in a covered pot in cooking liquid (less liquid and larger cuts of meat than a stew).
Stewing	Moist heat	Similar to braising, but stewing is the preferred method for small cubes of tough meat.	Meat is first browned at a high temperature, then simmered in a covered pot in cooking liquid (more liquid and smaller cuts of meat than braising).
Sous vide	Moist heat	Meat is gently cooked to the temperature of the water, so this method can be used on tender or tough cuts of meat.	Meat is sealed in a plastic bag and immersed in a heated water bath.

CURING SALTS

Curing salts are primarily used to prevent unwanted bacteria from growing on preserved meats, but they can also enhance the color, texture, and flavor of the meat. There are two types of Prague powder.

Prague Powder #1

AKA Pink Curing Salt #1, Insta Cure #1

Prague powder #1 is the most common type of curing salt. It's a mixture of salt and sodium nitrite, anticaking agents, and a bit of red dye to keep it from being confused with table salt. It can be found at butcher shops, specialty grocery stores, sporting goods stores that sell sausage making equipment, and on Amazon. It's designed for cures that take less than thirty days and are cooked, brined, smoked, or canned. This includes everything from poultry and fish to bacon, corned beef, and more. Be careful, as this powder can be dangerous if consumed in large quantities; use a food scale and be precise with measurements.

Most recipes call for 0.25 percent of the total weight of meat when applying Prague powder #1. To calculate the correct amount, take the weight of the meat in grams and multiply by 0.0025. This will give you the weight in grams of Prague powder #1 that is needed.

Example:

Pork belly weighs 2,268 grams (5 pounds; 2.3 kg)

2,268 x 0.0025 = 5.67 grams of Prague powder #1

Prague Powder #2

AKA Pink Curing Salt #2, Insta Cure #2

Prague powder #2 is a mixture of salt and sodium nitrate (different than sodium *nitrite*). It is used on meats that are air dried and not cooked, as the nitrates break down into nitrites overtime and remain active for months. Think prosciutto, bresaola, and dry-cured salami.

Use the same instructions for Prague powder #2 as those given above for Prague powder #1.

FREEZING MEAT

Air is your enemy when it comes to the freezer. Cold, dry air coming into contact with meat causes the outer layers to lose moisture and harden, creating ice crystals that indicate freezer burn. To prevent this, air should be kept from touching the meat.

As a hunter, I've put hundreds of pounds of meat in the freezer over the years. These are my two favorite methods for freezing meat effectively.

Vacuum Sealer

A vacuum sealer pulls air out of the bag and seals it tight so no air or moisture can get in. In my opinion this is the best method for freezing meat. These bags can be somewhat delicate in the freezer, so be sure to handle with care to avoid accidently puncturing holes in the bag.

Plastic Wrap and Freezer Paper

The second method I use frequently is a combination of plastic wrap and freezer paper. First, I wrap the meat tightly in plastic wrap, then I cover it in freezer paper with the waxy coated side toward the meat. Secure with a piece of tape and label with a marker.

BUTCHERY

Animals are divided into large cuts called primals, such as the ham of a pig or the front shoulder of a deer. These can be broken into smaller cuts, called subprimals, such as the drumstick from a chicken leg or the eye of round from the hindquarter of a deer.

Every cut of meat has its own special requirements for preparation. Some cuts, like the backstrap of a deer, are best enjoyed as medium-rare steaks, while others, like the picnic roast from a pig's front shoulder, should be slowly cooked at low temperatures until the meat falls apart into delightful shredded bites.

A center-cut pork chop, for example, is succulently tender and very lean relative to other cuts of pork. Cut from the center of the loin, this pork chop is evenly shaped and is best prepared using a hot-and-fast cooking method. The shank of a deer, on the other hand, is the least tender cut on the entire animal. Riddled with tough tendons and connective tissue, the shank requires a low-and-slow cooking method like braising to transform it into tender bites and unlock the flavor trapped within the bone.

Chicken

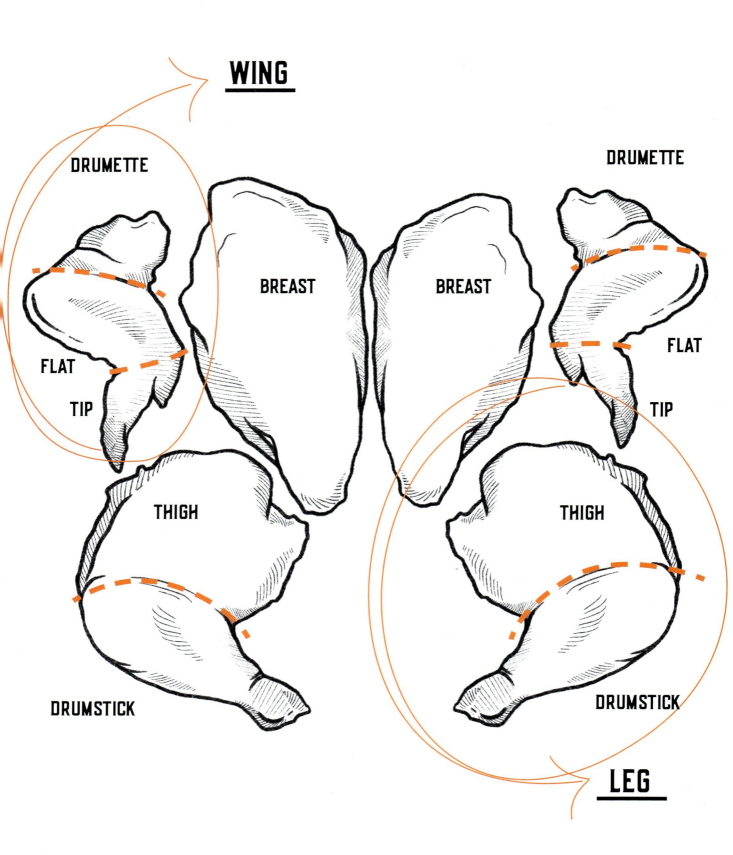

WING

DRUMETTE

DRUMETTE

BREAST

BREAST

FLAT

FLAT

TIP

TIP

THIGH

THIGH

DRUMSTICK

DRUMSTICK

LEG

CHICKEN CUTS EXPLAINED

WHOLE BIRD

Because of their small stature, chickens are fantastic to roast whole. The fat from the skin renders down to flavor and moisten the meat as it cooks. Even cooking is the challenge when roasting the whole bird, as it might end up partially pink and underdone, or partially overcooked and dry. It's important to monitor the meat's internal temperature closely. Look for the liquids to turn clear when pierced with a fork or knife. If you find the breast meat is browning too quickly, place a tent of aluminum foil over that portion of the chicken.

WINGS

The wings can be broken down into three cuts: the drumette, the flat, and the tip. The drumette and flat contain flavorful skin, bones, and a small amount of meat. They are best fried or baked in the oven and go well with a variety of flavors, including everything from garlic Parmesan and mango habanero to classic buffalo. If you're not a fan of wings, they make a great addition to homemade chicken stock.

LEGS

The legs are formed by two cuts, the thigh and the drumstick. Some of the darkest, most flavorful meat on the bird comes from the legs. They can be prepared whole, keeping the thigh and drumsticks together, or cooked separate. I prefer cooking the legs bone in, with the skin on to provide as much depth in flavor as possible. Chicken legs are forgiving in the sense that they tend to stay moist even when overcooked.

BREAST MEAT

Chicken breasts are ubiquitous in North American cooking and certainly one of the most common cuts of meat found in American households. Chicken breasts are light, tender, and mildly flavored, but they are susceptible to overcooking and drying out. Cooking chicken breasts to an internal temperature of 165°F (74°C) helps create the juiciest meat possible.

TENDERLOINS

The tenderloins, or tenders, are exactly like what they sound like: tender strips of chicken. These long, slender strips of meat are found attached to the underside of the chicken breast. Their shape makes them perfect as finger food, on skewers, or as the meat used in stir-fries. Like breast meat, the tenders are light meat that is mildly flavored and easy to overcook, causing them to dry out.

BONES

There's more than meets the eye when it comes to the bones of a chicken. They're loaded with rich flavor that can only be unlocked by cooking them slowly for hours until the collagen and tissues break down. Every bone from the carcass can and should be used to make chicken stock or to flavor soups and stews.

HOW TO BUTCHER A CHICKEN

It can be intimidating to butcher an animal for the first time. Luckily, for anyone new to the art of butchery, chicken is the perfect place to start. Chickens are small enough to fit on your countertop cutting board and are easily accessible. Fresh chicken is easy to come by: You may even have a neighbor who raises chickens. Most home cooks have some experience cutting and cooking it, and the stakes are fairly low. (It's okay if there is a little extra breast meat left on the rib cage.)

TOOLS NEEDED

Boning knife (see page 16 for more on knives)
Honing rod
Large cutting board
Poultry shears

1. **Remove the wings:** With the bird on its back and the head end pointed toward you, locate the shoulder joint of the wing. Using your fingers, feel for the joint where the wing bones meet the body of the bird. Hold the wing away from the body to better expose the joint. For added precision, use the tip of your boning knife to cut through the joint until you feel the wing pop out of its socket. Continue cutting to separate the wing from the body, avoiding cutting through the breast meat. Repeat to remove the other wing.

2. **Remove the legs:** With the bird on its back, hold the leg away from the body to expose the hip joint. Using your knife, cut through the taut skin between the leg and the breast (see illustration 2a). If you plan to keep the skin on the breast, take extra care to hold the skin on the breast in place while making this first cut. Continue cutting until your knife hits the hard ball-and-socket joint of the hip. To dislocate the joint (see illustration 2b), use leverage by bending the leg back and away from the body until you feel a pop. Flip the bird over and cut the leg away from the pelvis: You're using the bones of the pelvis as a guide to carve the meat away from the carcass.

   Note: Keep an eye out for the tiny but flavorful "oyster meat." This is located on the back of the bird in a small, circular oyster-like depression. You might miss it the first time you butcher a chicken, but it's worth looking for: When you find it, use your knife to carve it out as you remove the leg.

3. **Remove the breast meat – Option 1, Bone-in Split Breast.** Set the bird on its neck end and cut along the edge of the pelvic girdle to separate the backbone from the rest of the bird (see illustration 3a). Use poultry shears to cut all the way down both sides of the spine until the back completely separates from the rib cage and breast meat (see illustration 3b). Place the breast skin-side down, then use your knife to split the center bone with a forceful chopping motion (see illustration 3c). (This is the sternum bone, often called the kneel bone: a long and slender bone found in the center of the breasts.) Continue cutting through the meat to separate the breasts into two bone-in pieces.

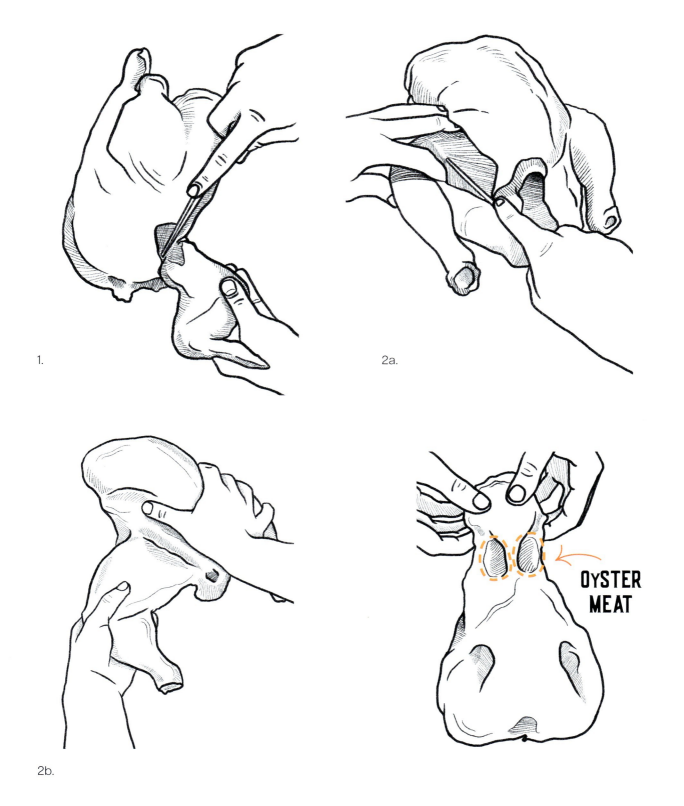

1.

2a.

2b.

OYSTER MEAT

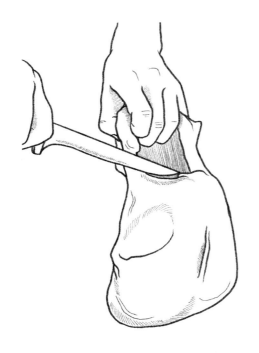

3a.

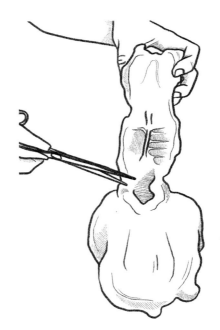

3b.

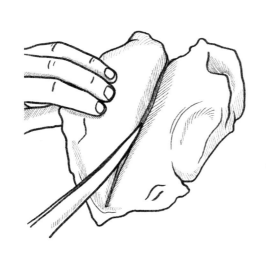

3c.

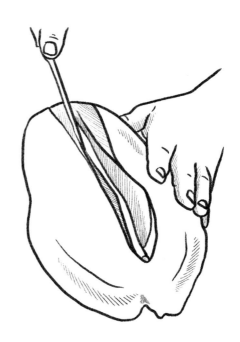

3d.

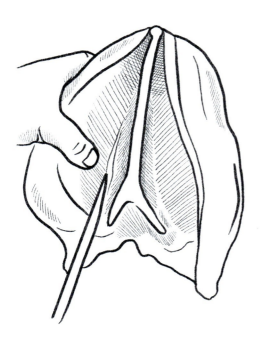

3e.

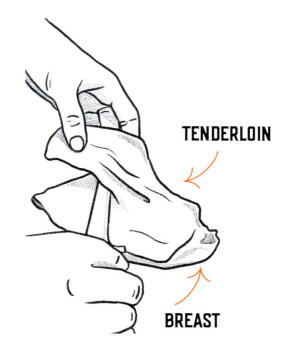

TENDERLOIN

BREAST

4.

Remove the breast meat – Option 2, Boneless breast. Set the bird on its back and locate the kneel bone with your fingertips. Keeping your knife blade turned inward toward the bone, make a long cut down the side of the kneel bone. Repeat on the other side of the bone, making sure to turn your knife blade toward the bone again (see illustration 3d). At the top of the breast, retrace your initial cut until you hit the wishbone. Trace the wishbone downward about 1 inch (2.5 cm). Repeat on the other side. Peel the breast away from the carcass with one hand and fillet the meat off the rib cage.

Make cuts where the meat and the bone meet. As you pull the breast back, more meat will come off the rib cage and you'll see the next place to cut (see illustration 3e). Continue until the breast is fully released from the carcass. Repeat with the opposite breast.

4. **Remove the tenderloin (boneless breast only):** The tenderloin is a long, slender piece of meat that sits on the underside of the breast meat. Place the boneless breast upside-down and peel the tenderloin away from the breast using your knife.

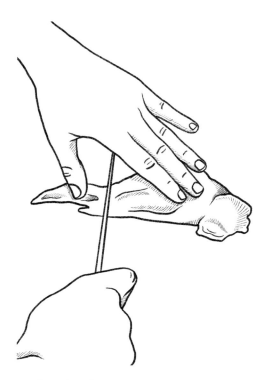

Remove the wing tips.

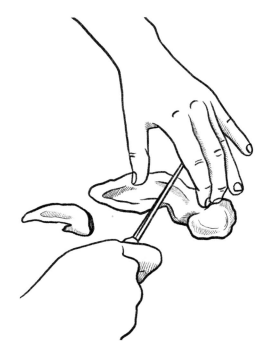

Separate the drumette from the flat.

Going Further

- **Skinning.** It's easier to remove the skin from the breast before you cut the meat away from the bone. Put down the knife and grab a paper towel: Skin is best removed with your hands, but meat can be slimy and slippery. A paper towel provides enough grip to pull the skin away from the meat.

EXTRAS TO SAVE

Save the tips of wings, back, rib cage, and any other bones removed for stock (see page 75).

- **Separating drumette from flat.** Feel for the gap in the joint between the drumette, the section closest to the bird, and the flat, which is the middle section. With your knife parallel to the cutting board, use downward pressure to complete the separation right where the bones meet in the gap of the joint. If you feel resistance, don't continue pressing: Reset and try a different angle until you cut through without resistance. Repeat this step to separate the tip from the flat.

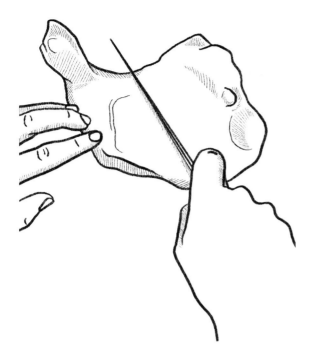

Separate the drumstick from the thigh.

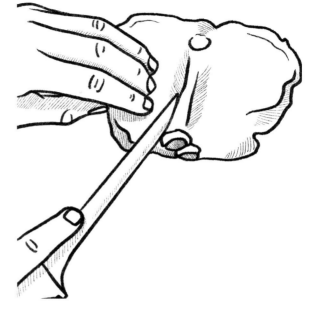

Remove the bone from the thigh.

- **Separating drumstick from thigh.** Feel with your fingers to locate the gap in the joint between the drumstick and the thigh. If you plan to leave the skin on, be sure to cut from the skin side. With your knife parallel to the cutting board, use downward pressure to complete the separation right where the bones meet in the gap of the joint. If you feel resistance, don't continue pressing: Reset and try a different angle until you cut through without resistance.

- **Boneless thighs.** After separating the thigh from the drumstick, place the thigh skin-side down on the cutting board. Locate the femur bone with your fingers and cut along both sides of the edge of the bone. Cut 360 degrees around the tip of the ball-and-socket joint. Using your fingers, lift the bone away from the meat as you cut all around the bone until it completely releases from the thigh meat.

- **Ground meat.** Meat from any part of the chicken can be used for ground meat. Be sure to remove all skin and bones before grinding.

MAPLE-ROASTED CHICKEN WITH AUTUMN VEGETABLES

Roasting anything whole may sound like it would be a lot of fuss, but it can actually be about as hands-off as it gets. It starts with a brine, which seasons the meat overnight, infusing it with rich flavors of fresh thyme and garlic. Then your roasting pan does most of the work as the bird slowly roasts, creating the perfect environment for even cooking and golden browning.

This recipe is one of the best ways to enjoy an entire chicken. I love the way it combines the beauty of seasonal ingredients to pair perfectly with juicy, slow-roasted chicken that's ready to share.

Instructions

1. Create the brine. In the largest stockpot you can find, boil 1 quart (1 L) of water, honey, thyme, garlic, salt, and pepper. Add the remaining 2 quarts (1.9 L) of cold water and allow the brine to cool down to room temperature.

2. Wait for the brine to cool completely. It is important for it to be *cold* (see note below). Place the chicken in the brine, cover, and refrigerate for 12 to 24 hours.

    Note: Do not put the chicken into the brine until it has cooled completely or else the hot water will begin to cook the meat.

3. Thirty minutes prior to cooking, remove the chicken from the brine. Pat it dry with paper towels and set it on the countertop, allowing it to come to room temperature. This is an important step, as it will ensure even cooking. Strain the brine, setting aside the thyme and garlic. Dry the thyme and garlic with paper towels, then stuff them into the cavity of the bird, along with both lemon halves.

4. Preheat the oven to 400°F (204°C).

INGREDIENTS

For the brine:

3 quarts (2.8 L) water, separated

1 cup (340 g) honey

1 bunch thyme, about 10 sprigs

1 head of garlic, halved crosswise

¾ cup (177 g) kosher salt

2 tablespoons (10 g) black peppercorn

For the chicken:

1 whole chicken (5 to 6 pounds; 2.3 to 2.7 kg)

1 lemon, halved

For the vegetables:

1 medium acorn squash, cut into ½-inch (1-cm) slices

4 rainbow carrots, peeled and thickly chopped (see note)

1 medium onion, thickly sliced

Olive oil, for drizzling

Kosher salt and freshly ground black pepper to taste

⅔ cup (158 g) unsalted butter, melted and divided

2 tablespoons (40 g) maple syrup

Prep Time: 20 minutes plus 12- to 24-hour tenderizing

Cook Time: 1 hour 30 minutes

Yield: Serves 6 to 8

Continued

5. Truss the chicken. Position the bird breast-side up with the legs facing you. Pull the legs together while pushing the breast meat up. Expose as much of the skin on the breast as possible. Using twine, tie the legs together tightly. Tuck the tips of both wings back and underneath the body of the bird. There are fancier ways to truss a chicken, but I prefer to keep it simple.

6. In a roasting pan, place the acorn squash, carrots, and onion, then lightly drizzle with olive oil and season with kosher salt and freshly ground black pepper. Stir with a spatula or wooden spoon to distribute the oil and seasoning evenly, then position the vegetables closely together with thicker pieces toward the outer edges of the pan (this will help to avoid charring). The chicken juices will run off onto the vegetables as the bird cooks, so don't add too much olive oil.

7. Place a roasting rack on top of the vegetables. Place the chicken breast-side up on the rack and brush the chicken with half of the melted butter. Sprinkle with kosher salt and freshly ground black pepper. Place in the oven.

8. After 45 minutes, combine the remaining melted butter with the maple syrup and brush it on the chicken. Rotate the pan and cook for an additional 35 to 45 minutes, until the skin is golden brown, the juices run clear, and the internal temperature of the chicken has reached 165°F (74°C).

   Note: Keep checking the chicken as it cooks. If the skin is becoming too brown, too quickly, cover it with aluminum foil.

9. Allow chicken to rest for 15 to 20 minutes. Carve and serve with vegetables.

   Note: Rainbow carrots are a feast for the eyes, with shades of purple, vibrant yellow, and maroon. When cooked, though, there's virtually no difference in taste compared to regular carrots. It's okay to use standard orange carrots if you can't find (or don't want to pay extra for) rainbow carrots.

   TIP: Save the chicken carcass to make stock (recipe on page 75).

OVEN-BAKED GARLIC-PARMESAN CHICKEN WINGS

There's something about a smoky dive bar that I find charming. The dark, grungy room, the crack of pool balls colliding, and even the at times questionable crowd all add up to a vivid, unique experience. Then again, maybe I love dive bars because some of the best wings I've ever had were served in these under-the-radar kitchens.

This recipe was inspired by my go-to chicken wing order: savory Parmesan wings. Naturally, I recommend pairing this recipe with a tall, cold beer.

Instructions

1. Salt the chicken wings liberally with kosher salt. Cover and place in the refrigerator for 12 to 24 hours. Salting the meat in advance makes a big difference in flavor and tenderness. (See page 22 for more information.)

2. About 30 minutes prior to cooking, remove the chicken wings from the refrigerator and allow them to come to room temperature. This important step ensures even cooking.

3. Preheat the oven to 425°F (118°C). Line a baking sheet with aluminum foil and place a wire baking rack on top.

4. Use paper towels to pat dry the chicken wings. This aids in crisping the skin.

5. Place the chicken in a large bowl, then add the avocado oil and mix until well coated.

6. In a small bowl, combine the cornstarch, black pepper, onion powder, garlic powder, smoked paprika, and 1 teaspoon kosher salt.

7. Add the spice mix to the large bowl and combine until the chicken is evenly covered in the seasoning. I like to use my hands for this step because I'm better able to coat the chicken, which ensures that every bite is equally flavorful.

Continued

INGREDIENTS

For the chicken wings:

2 to 3 pounds (900 g to 1.4 kg) bone-in chicken wings, separated and tips removed

2 tablespoons (30 ml) avocado oil

2 tablespoons (16 g) cornstarch

1 tablespoon (6 g) black pepper

1 tablespoon (7 g) onion powder

1 tablespoon (9 g) garlic powder

1 tablespoon (7 g) smoked paprika

1 teaspoon kosher salt, plus more for tenderizing the wings

Continued

8. Place the chicken wings on the baking rack. Be sure they are evenly spaced and do not touch.

   Note: The baking rack helps create a crispy skin and is worth the small investment if you don't already own one.

9. Bake the chicken for 25 to 30 minutes, flipping halfway through to cook evenly on both sides. The chicken is done cooking when the juices run clear when pierced with a fork.

10. Remove the chicken from the oven and place the top oven rack in its highest position. Set the oven to a high broil and place the chicken on the top rack for about 1 minute. Keep a close watch on the chicken during this step: Every oven is different and I've accidentally torched wings just by turning my attention to something else for 20 seconds! You're looking for a dark brown kiss of color with a slight char in places. Flip and repeat on the other side.

11. Remove the chicken from the oven and allow the wings to rest.

12. To make the sauce, melt the butter in a small pan over low heat. Stir in the minced garlic and cook until the garlic is fragrant, about 1 minute. Don't allow the garlic to brown. Remove from the heat and stir in the parsley.

13. Add the chicken to a large bowl and pour the sauce over the wings. Toss until the chicken is well coated. Add the grated Parmesan cheese and continue tossing. It's important to add the butter-garlic sauce to the wings, then add the cheese. If you add the cheese to the hot butter directly, it will become a thick mess and won't adhere properly to the wings.

14. Garnish the wings with additional parsley and cheese and serve with blue cheese or ranch dressing for dipping.

For the garlic-Parmesan sauce:

1 stick (112 g) unsalted butter

3 tablespoons (30 g) minced garlic

½ cup (52 g) grated Parmesan cheese

2 tablespoons (44 ml) chopped fresh parsley

For serving:

Grated Parmesan cheese

Chopped fresh parsley

Blue cheese or ranch dressing for dipping

Optional: Carrots or celery

Prep Time: 10 minutes plus 12- to 24-hour tenderizing

Cook Time: 35 minutes

Yield: Serves 4

CHERRY ALMOND CHICKEN SALAD

Chicken legs hold more flavor than any other part of the bird and are extremely forgiving when it comes to cooking because they don't dry out as easily as other cuts. Braised chicken legs are easy to shred, making them perfect for salads, tacos, and sandwiches.

This salad is tart from the cherries, bitter from the arugula, creamy from the goat cheese, and crunchy from the toasted almonds. It's one of my all-time favorite chicken salad recipes.

Dried Cherries on the Trail

My mom, sister, and I backpacked a portion of the Appalachian Trail in 2018. For five days we slept in tents that were carried on our backs, filtered drinking water from freshwater springs, and ate bland dehydrated meals.

There's no room for luxuries on a hiking trip like this, so as we went, finding small things to enjoy felt like big wins. I treasured the dried cherries we'd packed to snack on during the hike. The soft, chewy texture and sweet burst of energy were uplifting every time I started to slump.

None of the meals we ate during that trip were as good as this recipe, but the way those dried cherries tasted on the trail comes close. And I think of how glorious they were with every bite of this delicious salad.

INGREDIENTS

For the chicken:

6 chicken legs (skin-on, bone-in thigh and drumsticks)

Kosher salt and black pepper for seasoning

4 tablespoons (59 ml) olive oil, separated

¾ cup (177 ml) dry white wine

2 medium yellow onions, peeled and quartered

2 cups (474 ml) chicken stock

For the salad:

2 cups (475 ml) water

1 cup (160 g) wild rice, uncooked

Kosher salt, to taste

1 tablespoon (14 g) unsalted butter

2 giant handfuls arugula, roughly chopped

3½ ounces (100 g) goat cheese, crumbled

¾ cup (82 g) dried cherries, sweetened

¾ cup (177 g) almonds, roasted, salted, and roughly chopped

Continued

Instructions

1. Salt the chicken liberally with kosher salt. Wrap tightly with plastic wrap and place in the refrigerator for 12 to 24 hours. Salt applied to the meat in advance makes a big difference in flavor and tenderness. (See page 22 for more information.)

Continued

2. Thirty minutes prior to cooking, remove the chicken from the refrigerator and allow it to come to room temperature. This important step ensures even cooking.

3. Preheat the oven to 450°F (232°C). Heat a cast-iron skillet over medium-high heat.

4. Dry the chicken legs thoroughly with paper towels.

5. Add 2 tablespoons (30 ml) of olive oil to the skillet. When the oil just barely smokes, add the chicken thighs, skin down. Cook for 4 to 5 minutes without touching the meat, allowing the skin to develop a brown crust. Flip and cook for another 4 to 5 minutes.

6. Remove the chicken from the pan and lower the heat to medium.

7. Deglaze the pan with the white wine, using a wooden spoon to scrape the bottom of the pan and release any brown bits. Pour this liquid into a small bowl and set aside for later.

8. Return the pan to medium-high heat and add 2 tablespoons (30 ml) of fresh olive oil. Put quartered onions face down and allow to sear for 4 minutes. Again, to create a brown crust, don't touch the onions while they're searing.

9. Place the chicken legs on top of the onions. Pour the reserved glazing liquid and enough chicken stock to cover only the bottom fourth of the chicken legs (roughly 2 cups [474 ml], but it completely depends on the size of your pan).

10. Bake for 5 minutes at 450°F (232°C), then reduce the oven temperature to 325°F (163°C). Cook for 30 to 40 minutes, until the chicken is tender.

11. While the chicken is braising, cook the rice. In a small pot, combine the water and wild rice and bring to a boil. Cover and reduce to a simmer for about 30 minutes or until the rice is tender. Season with salt and butter. Set aside to cool.

12. Remove the chicken and a quarter of the onions from the skillet and set aside. Discard the remaining onions and liquid. Once cool enough to handle, use your hands or two forks to shred the chicken. Thinly slice the onion and set aside for garnish.

13. In a medium bowl, combine the white wine vinegar, olive oil, garlic, and sugar. Add kosher salt and black pepper to desired taste.

14. To assemble the salad, fill a serving bowl with the wild rice, arugula, chicken, goat cheese, cherries, almonds, and onions. Toss with dressing and serve immediately.

For the dressing:

2 tablespoons (30 ml) white wine vinegar

6 tablespoons (89 ml) extra virgin olive oil

½ teaspoon garlic, minced

1 teaspoon granulated sugar

Kosher salt and black pepper to taste

Prep Time: 15 minutes plus 12- to 24-hour tenderizing
Cook Time: 50 minutes
Yield: Serves 4 to 6 people

OVEN-ROASTED MANGO DRUMSTICKS

Fruit is an unexpected ingredient to add to savory meats, yet the combination is intoxicating. Fruit adds sweetness, tartness, texture, and flavor to otherwise one-note savory dishes. You'll find fruit prepared with meat throughout this book, like in my Cherry Almond Chicken Salad recipe on page 50 or my Reverse Seared Pork Chops with Apple Relish recipe on page 98.

This chicken drumstick recipe uses plump golden mangos to create a sweet, tangy sauce that lightly glazes the chicken and caramelizes as the drumsticks broil to crispy perfection.

Because drumsticks have a high fat content, preparing them with the skin on locks in the fat, which provides flavorful juice for moist, tender meat. The combination of yogurt and lime juice in the marinade helps further tenderize the meat and season it from within.

Instructions

1. In a medium bowl, combine the marinade spices, minced ginger, minced garlic, Greek yogurt, lime zest, lime juice, vegetable oil, and kosher salt.

2. Use a sharp knife to score each drumstick a few times to increase the surface area and allow the marinade to better penetrate the meat. Place the drumsticks in a resealable plastic bag.

3. Pour the marinade over the chicken and massage to completely coat the meat. Refrigerate overnight to increase flavor and tenderness.

4. Thirty minutes prior to cooking, remove the chicken from the refrigerator, rinse the drumsticks, and pat dry. With an overnight marinade, the flavors work their way into the meat and so any remaining marinade can be rinsed away without removing flavor. It's important that the drumsticks be dried well with a paper towel prior to cooking to create a crispy skin in the oven.

Continued

INGREDIENTS

For the marinade:

1 tablespoon (7 g) paprika

1 tablespoon (7 g) ground cumin

1 tablespoon (6 g) ground coriander

½ teaspoon cayenne pepper

1 tablespoon (6 g) minced ginger

6 garlic cloves, minced

¼ cup (63 g) whole milk Greek yogurt

1 teaspoon lime zest

2 tablespoons (30 ml) lime juice

¼ cup (55 ml) vegetable oil

2½ teaspoons (20 g) kosher salt

12 chicken drumsticks

Continued

5.   Lightly season the meat with kosher salt and allow the drumsticks to come to room temperature. This important step ensures even cooking.

6.   Preheat the oven to 450°F (232°C). Place an oven-proof wire rack on top of a baking sheet.

7.   Space the drumsticks evenly on the wire rack, making sure not to overcrowd them. Bake for 45 minutes, turning once halfway through.

8.   While the chicken is cooking, pour the rice wine vinegar, water, and sugar in a saucepan and stir over medium heat until the sugar is dissolved. Add the jalapeño, ginger, and mango and cook on medium-low heat for about 10 minutes, until the mangoes soften and the liquid thickens slightly. Remove from heat and add the lime juice. Stir to combine.

9.   Transfer the mixture to a food processor or blender and purée until smooth. Set aside until the drumsticks are cooked.

10. Remove the drumsticks from the oven and turn the oven to broil. Brush the drumsticks on all sides with the mango sauce. Return the drumsticks to the oven and broil for an additional 5 minutes, turning halfway through, until the skin is crisp and a bit charred.

> **Note:** Keep a very close watch on the chicken as they broil. Every oven is different and I've accidentally torched drumsticks by turning my attention to something else for 20 seconds!

11. Garnish the drumsticks with chopped cilantro. Serve with lime wedges and the remaining mango sauce for dipping.

For the mango sauce:
   ¾ cup (174 ml) rice wine vinegar
   ¼ cup (59 ml) water
   ¼ cup (49 g) sugar
   1 tablespoon (11 g) minced jalapeño
   1½ teaspoons minced ginger
   1 ripe mango, chopped
   2 tablespoons (30 ml) lime juice

For serving:
   Cilantro, chopped
   Lime wedges

Prep Time: 20 minutes plus 24-hour marinade
Cook Time: 50 minutes
Yield: Serves 4 to 6

FRESH ENGLISH PEA AND CHICKEN THIGH SOUP

As pleasant as walking barefoot in the soft grass, this soup is simple and brings me joy with every bite. It is light but filling, which makes it just as appealing to eat in the summertime as in the winter.

This soup shines with sweet bursts of English peas, an earthy grounding of cremini mushrooms, and a robust chicken flavor thanks to homemade chicken stock (recipe on page 75). I like to eat this soup with crusty bread or buttery crackers.

Instructions

1. Salt the chicken thighs liberally with kosher salt. Cover and place in the refrigerator for 12 to 24 hours. Salt applied to the meat in advance makes a big difference in flavor and tenderness. (See page 22 for more information.)

2. About 30 minutes prior to cooking, remove the chicken from the refrigerator and allow it to come to room temperature. This important step ensures even cooking. During this time, trim any excess fat from the chicken and pat the meat dry with paper towels.

3. Heat a Dutch oven over medium-high heat. Once hot, heat 2 tablespoons (30 ml) of olive oil until the oil flows like water when the pan is tilted.

4. Place the chicken thighs in the pan and sear one side for 4 minutes without touching or moving the chicken. Flip and sear the other side for 4 additional minutes, again without touching or moving the meat. The goal is to create a brown, crusty sear without cooking the thighs all the way through. Remove the chicken from the pan and set aside.

Continued

INGREDIENTS

1 to 2 pounds (0.5 to 0.9 kg) boneless, skinless chicken thighs

Kosher salt

4 tablespoons (59 ml) olive oil, divided

1 cup (130 g) diced carrots

1 cup (160 g) diced onion

1 cup (120 g) diced celery

2 cups (156 g) sliced cremini mushrooms, stems removed

1½ teaspoons freshly minced garlic

8 cups (1.9 L) chicken stock (page 75)

5 thyme sprigs, tied with twine

1 cup (150 g) shelled English peas

3 tablespoons (13 g) chopped fresh parsley

1 tablespoon (15 ml) white wine vinegar

Black pepper, to taste

Prep Time: 10 minutes plus 12- to 24-hour tenderizing
Cook Time: 35 minutes
Yield: Serves 6 to 8

5. Pour out any fat remaining in the pot, then add 2 tablespoons (30 ml) of olive oil. Sauté the carrots, onions, celery, and mushrooms, stirring occasionally until golden brown and soft, about 12 minutes. Season lightly with kosher salt and pepper. Add the garlic and sauté for 1 minute more.

6. Add the chicken stock and thyme to the pot. Scrape the bottom of the pot with a wooden spoon to release any brown bits.

7. Place the chicken back into the pot and bring it to a boil. Reduce the heat to low and simmer uncovered for about 30 minutes, until chicken is fork tender and shreds easily. Don't stir the soup as it simmers. If you notice fat collecting on the surface of the soup, gently skim it off and discard it.

8. Add the peas, parsley, and white wine vinegar. Simmer for 3 to 5 minutes, until the peas are tender but still bright in color.

9. Remove the pot from the heat and transfer the chicken to a cutting board or baking sheet to shred. I like to allow the chicken to cool for a few minutes before shredding it with my hands, but you can also use two forks to tear the meat into bite-sized pieces. Return the shredded chicken to the pot.

10. Remove the thyme bundle and discard. Season the soup with kosher salt and black pepper to taste. Garnish with fresh parsley and serve warm.

BONE-IN CHICKEN THIGHS WITH TANGY MUSTARD PAN SAUCE

Boneless chicken thighs are good, but bone-in chicken thighs offer a spectacular depth of flavor. A pan sauce helps hold on to as much of that flavor as possible by incorporating all the browned bits and drippings that accumulate during searing and roasting.

I love the combination of tangy Dijon mustard, creamy full-fat yogurt, and bitter spinach with the richness of dark bone-in thigh meat.

Instructions

1. Salt the chicken thighs liberally with kosher salt. Place in the refrigerator for 12 to 24 hours. Salt applied to the meat in advance makes a big difference in flavor and tenderness. (See page 22 for more information.)

2. About 30 minutes prior to cooking, remove the chicken from the refrigerator and allow it to come to room temperature. This important step ensures even cooking.

3. Preheat the oven to 400°F (204°C). Pat the chicken dry with paper towels, then season lightly with freshly ground black pepper.

4. Heat a large oven-safe frying pan over medium-high heat. Once the pan is hot, add 1 tablespoon (15 ml) of oil and allow oil to heat until it flows like water when the pan is tilted.

5. Add the chicken to the hot oil skin-side down and sear for 5 minutes without touching or moving the chicken thighs. This creates a brown, crusty sear without cooking them all the way through.

Continued

INGREDIENTS

4 bone-in, skin-on chicken thighs

Kosher salt and freshly ground black pepper

2 tablespoons (30 ml) avocado oil, divided

1 large yellow onion, sliced thin

1½ teaspoons freshly minced garlic

⅔ cup (157 ml) dry white wine

1 teaspoon white wine vinegar

3 tablespoons (45 g) cream cheese

3 tablespoons (45 g) plain full fat yogurt

¼ cup (52 g) high-quality Dijon mustard

2 tablespoons (28 g) unsalted butter

4 ounces (114 g) fresh spinach

Chopped fresh parsley, for garnish

Prep Time: 10 minutes plus 12- to 24-hour tenderizing

Cook Time: 20 minutes

Yield: Serves 2 to 3

6.   Flip the chicken thighs and move the skillet into the preheated oven. Cook uncovered for 15 to 20 minutes until the chicken reaches an internal temperature of 165°F (74°C). Remove the chicken from the pan and set aside.

7.   Pour out any fat remaining in the pan, then add the remaining 1 tablespoon (15 ml) of oil. Once the oil is hot, add the onions and sauté until slightly brown and translucent, about 15 minutes. Add the garlic and sauté for about 1 minute, until fragrant.

8.   Pour in the wine, then use a wooden spoon to scrape the brown bits off the bottom of the pan. Add the white wine vinegar and allow to reduce to a thicker consistency.

9.   Whisk in the yogurt, cream cheese, Dijon mustard, and butter. Whisk vigorously until well combined. Bring to a rolling boil, then reduce to a simmer.

10.   Add the spinach and cook until wilted, about 2 minutes.

11.   Serve the sauce and spinach over the chicken. Garnish with parsley.

ONE-BOWL SPICY CURRIED CHICKEN SALAD

A whole, bone-in chicken breast is heart shaped. Splitting this in half creates two bone-in chicken breasts, called split chicken breasts. Because they include the bone, split chicken breasts are fantastic for roasting. The bone provides flavor and allows the meat to cook more evenly. The skin creates a natural moisture blanket that helps keep the meat juicy and tender.

This salad pairs this delicious cut of chicken with crunchy pistachios, sweet golden raisins, and fresh celery. It's a lovely way to dress up roasted chicken without hiding it. Serve on toasted slices of crusty bread, wrapped in leaves of butter lettuce, or with crunchy crackers or cucumbers.

Instructions

1. Salt the chicken liberally with kosher salt. Wrap tightly with plastic wrap and place in the refrigerator for 12 to 24 hours. Salt applied to the meat in advance makes a big difference in flavor and tenderness. (Learn more on page 22.)

2. Thirty minutes prior to cooking, remove the chicken from the refrigerator and allow it to come to room temperature. This important step ensures even cooking.

3. Preheat the oven to 350°F (177°C).

4. Place the chicken on a rimmed baking sheet. Drizzle each breast with 1 teaspoon of avocado oil. Season generously with kosher salt and freshly ground black pepper.

5. Bake for 40 to 45 minutes, or until the internal temperature of the chicken has reached 160°F (71°C). Allow it to rest for about 20 minutes, during which time the chicken will continue to cook.

6. In a large bowl, combine the mayonnaise, Greek yogurt, honey, curry powder, garlic, and cayenne pepper until smooth. Set aside for later.

INGREDIENTS

2 skin-on split chicken breasts

Kosher salt

2 teaspoons avocado oil, divided

Freshly ground black pepper

¼ cup (54 g) mayonnaise

¼ cup (62.7 g) plain, full-fat Greek yogurt

1 tablespoon (20 g) honey

¾ teaspoon curry powder

¼ teaspoon minced garlic

¼ teaspoon cayenne powder

½ cup (72 g) roughly chopped golden raisins

½ cup (64 g) roughly chopped roasted, salted pistachios, shells off

2 celery stalks, finely chopped

2 green onions, finely chopped

1 tablespoon (15 ml) freshly squeezed lemon juice

Prep Time: 20 minutes plus 12- to 24-hour tenderizing

Cook Time: 45 minutes

Yield: Serves 4

7. Once the chicken is done resting, remove the skin and use two forks or your hands to shred into bite-sized pieces.

8. In the bowl with the mayonnaise mixture, add the raisins, pistachios, celery, and green onions. Stir in the shredded chicken and mix until it is well coated with the sauce.

9. Stir in the lemon juice, then add kosher salt and black pepper to taste.

PAN-SEARED CHICKEN BREAST WITH PEANUT SAUCE AND BRIGHT SLAW

If pad thai is your go-to order at a Thai restaurant, you'll love this peanut sauce. It's packed with sweet and savory flavors like brown sugar, soy sauce, and, of course, peanut butter. Chicken breasts are naturally tender, with a mild taste, making them an excellent vehicle for bold flavors. They're the perfect choice for this creamy sauce, tangy slaw combo.

To achieve optimal results, it's important to salt the meat in advance—this adds flavor and tenderness—then pound the meat into an even layer. Watch the meat closely during cooking to keep it from getting overdone. This dish is best served with buttered and salted jasmine rice.

Instructions

1. Salt the chicken liberally with kosher salt. Wrap tightly with plastic wrap and place in the refrigerator for 12 to 24 hours. Salt applied to the meat in advance makes a big difference in flavor and tenderness. (See page 22 for more information.)

2. Thirty minutes prior to cooking, remove the chicken from the refrigerator and allow it to come to room temperature. This important step ensures even cooking.

3. In a medium bowl, whisk together the peanut butter, ginger, garlic, soy sauce, brown sugar, apple cider vinegar, sriracha, green onions, and water until well combined. Set aside.

4. Keep the chicken breasts wrapped in plastic and pound with a meat mallet or rolling pin until the meat is an even thickness, about ½ inch (1.3 cm) thick. Remove the meat from the plastic wrap and pat dry with paper towels.

Continued

INGREDIENTS

For the chicken:

4 boneless, skinless chicken breasts

Kosher salt

2 tablespoons (30 ml) avocado oil

For the sauce:

½ cup (129 g) peanut butter

2 tablespoons (12 g) minced ginger

2 tablespoons (20 g) minced garlic

3 tablespoons (42 ml) low-sodium soy sauce

¼ cup (59 g) light brown sugar

2 teaspoons apple cider vinegar

2 tablespoons (30 g) sriracha

4 green onions, whites only, thinly sliced

⅓ cup (79 ml) water

Continued

5. Heat a large pan over medium-high heat. Once the pan is hot, add the avocado oil.

6. When the oil is hot, about 30 seconds, place the chicken breasts in the pan and, without touching or moving the meat, sear one side for 5 minutes. Flip and sear the other side for 5 additional minutes, again without touching or moving the meat. Reduce heat to low, and flip the chicken breasts one more time.

7. Pour the sauce into pan, stirring with a wooden spoon or spatula. Once the sauce comes to a simmer, remove the pan from the heat and let rest for 5 minutes.

8. In a large bowl, combine the cabbage, carrot, green onions, cilantro, apple, apple cider vinegar, sesame oil, sesame seeds, honey, and peanut butter. Season with kosher salt as needed.

9. Serve the chicken with peanut sauce over jasmine rice with slaw on top or as a side. Garnish with roasted peanuts.

For the slaw:

¼ red cabbage, shredded

1 large carrot, peeled and shredded

3 green onions, thinly sliced

½ cup (9 g) chopped cilantro

1 apple, peeled and diced

½ cup (118 ml) apple cider vinegar

2 tablespoons (30 ml) sesame oil

3 tablespoons (35 g) toasted sesame seeds

3 tablespoons (59 g) honey

1 tablespoon (16 g) peanut butter

Kosher salt to taste

¼ cup (35 g) chopped roasted, salted peanuts, for garnish

Prep Time: 30 minutes plus 12- to 24-hour tenderizing

Cook Time: 20 minutes

Yield: Serves 4

BUFFALO CHICKEN TENDER WRAP

The chicken tender is one of America's most loved cuts of chicken—especially when breaded, fried, and served out of a fast-food restaurant window. When I make chicken tenders at home, I add hot sauce to satisfy my husband's love of heat and bake them to a golden-brown finish. They're versatile and can be enjoyed on their own, in a salad, or in this savory wrap with a flavorful buttermilk buffalo sauce.

Instructions

1. Salt the chicken tenders liberally with kosher salt. Cover them tightly with plastic wrap and place in the refrigerator for 12 to 24 hours. Salt applied to the meat in advance makes a big difference in flavor and tenderness. (See page 22 for more information.)

2. Thirty minutes prior to cooking, remove the chicken from the refrigerator and allow it to come to room temperature. This important step ensures even cooking.

3. Preheat the oven to 350°F (177°C).

4. Spread the panko bread crumbs in a thin layer on a bare baking sheet. Bake for about 5 minutes, until the bread crumbs are lightly browned. Transfer to shallow plate and stir in the 1 teaspoon kosher salt.

5. Increase the oven temperature to 450°F (232°C). Prepare a baking sheet by coating it lightly with oil or cooking spray.

6. In a shallow, microwave-proof mixing bowl, melt the butter in the microwave, then whisk in the hot sauce.

7. Add the egg and garlic to the butter mixture and whisk until well combined.

8. Spread the all-purpose flour on a shallow plate for dredging. Place the egg mixture next to the dredging plate.

INGREDIENTS

For the chicken tenders:

1 pound (455 g) chicken tenders

1 cup (115 g) plain panko bread crumbs

1 teaspoon kosher salt, plus more for tenderizing

¼ cup (54 g) unsalted butter

¼ cup (54 ml) Frank's RedHot Sauce

1 egg

1 teaspoon minced garlic

⅓ cup (42 g) all-purpose flour

For the buttermilk buffalo sauce:

¼ cup (58 g) sour cream

¼ cup (63 g) plain whole Greek yogurt

½ cup (121 ml) buttermilk

1 teaspoon garlic powder

1 teaspoon dill

2 tablespoons (6 g) chives

1 tablespoon (15 ml) Frank's RedHot Sauce

Kosher salt to taste

Continued

Continued

9. Pat the tenders dry with paper towels, which will ensure crispy breading. Place the tenders on the other side of the dredging plate.

10. Place one chicken tender at a time in the flour, flipping to coat all sides. Shake to remove excess flour, then place the tender in the egg mixture, again flipping to coat the entire surface and allowing the excess to drip away. Next, put the tender in the toasted panko crumbs, patting the crumbs into the meat to be sure they adhere well. Place the breaded tender on the prepared baking sheet. Repeat with all tenders, keeping some space between each piece to avoid overcrowding and uneven cooking.

11. Place the baking sheet in the oven and bake for 15 to 18 minutes.

12. Meanwhile, in a medium bowl, whisk together sour cream, yogurt, garlic powder, dill, chives, hot sauce, and ¼ cup (60 ml) of buttermilk until well combined. Add an additional 1 tablespoon (15 ml) of buttermilk at a time until desired consistency is achieved.

13. Place a flour tortilla on a flat surface and layer the chicken, lettuce, cheese, and tomato on top. Fold in the sides of the tortilla and roll tight.

14. Heat a medium skillet over medium heat. Add the butter. Once the butter is melted, place the wrap in the pan and sear it until you achieve a golden-brown crust. Flip the wrap and then press it down as it sears to help create even browning.

15. Remove the wrap from the pan, slice in half at an angle, and serve with buttermilk buffalo sauce.

For the wrap:

Large flour tortillas

Romaine lettuce, chopped

Shredded pepper jack cheese

Chopped tomato

2 tablespoons (28 g) unsalted butter

Prep Time: 15 minutes plus 12- to 24-hour tenderizing

Cook Time: 15 minutes

Yield: Serves 4

SPICY CHICKEN MEATBALLS IN MARINARA SAUCE

Enjoying a recipe as leftovers every bit as much as the night you cooked the original meal is like striking gold. While I don't always have good things to say about leftovers, I happily reheat these meatballs and enjoy them until there's nothing left and it's time to make more.

The marinara sauce is what makes these meatballs extra special. The chili peppers add mild heat, while the star anise adds a subtle sweet licorice flavor.

Instructions

For the marinara sauce:

1. Place a large pot over medium heat. Add the olive oil to the pot and, once warm, sauté the onion, stirring frequently, until it becomes translucent and is lightly browned, about 10 to 15 minutes.

2. Add the garlic, parsley, and chili peppers. Sauté until the parsley is wilted, about 1 minute.

3. Add the tomatoes and their liquid, the star anise pod, and the bay leaf. Use a wooden spoon to crush the tomatoes.

4. Increase the heat to high and bring the mixture to a boil, then reduce the heat to low and simmer uncovered for 2 hours, stirring every 30 minutes or so.

5. Carefully transfer the warm sauce to a blender, removing the bay leaf and anise pod but leaving the chili peppers in. Blend for 30 seconds, or until smooth.

6. Season with kosher salt to taste.

Continued

INGREDIENTS

For the marinara sauce:

¼ cup (54 ml) olive oil

2 medium yellow onions, diced

2 teaspoons sliced garlic

½ bunch chopped fresh parsley

2 whole dried chili peppers, stems removed

1 (28-ounce/800 g) can San Marzano tomatoes in liquid

1 star anise pod

1 bay leaf

½ teaspoon kosher salt, more to taste

For the meatballs:

1 pound (455 g) ground chicken

1 teaspoon garlic powder

1 teaspoon black pepper

½ teaspoon onion powder

½ teaspoon oregano

½ teaspoon paprika

½ teaspoon red pepper flakes

1 large egg

1 teaspoon kosher salt

½ cup (53 g) panko bread crumbs

2 tablespoons (30 ml) olive oil

2 tablespoons (30 ml) water

Continued

For the meatballs:

1. About 30 minutes prior to cooking, remove the chicken from the refrigerator and allow it to come to room temperature. This important step ensures even cooking.

2. Preheat the oven to 400°F (204°C).

3. In a large bowl, mix the garlic powder, black pepper, onion powder, oregano, paprika, red pepper flakes, egg, salt, and bread crumbs until well combined. I use my hands to ensure it's evenly mixed. With your hands, take small clumps of meat and form them into golf ball–sized meatballs.

4. Heat a large, deep, oven-safe skillet over medium-high heat. Once the pan is hot, add the olive oil and work in batches to sear the meatballs. Place a few meatballs in the skillet and sear for 2 minutes without touching or moving them. Flip the meatballs and sear the other side for 2 additional minutes, again without touching or moving the meat. The goal is to create a brown crusty sear without cooking the meatballs all the way through. Set the seared meatballs aside and continue working in batches until all of the meatballs are seared.

5. Deglaze the pan with the water, using a wooden spoon to scrape the brown bits from the bottom of the pan. Pour in the marinara sauce and stir.

6. Add the meatballs back to the pan and place in the preheated oven. Bake for 15 to 17 minutes.

7. Remove the pan from the oven and immediately grate Parmesan cheese over the top of the meatballs. Garnish with freshly chopped parsley and basil before serving.

For garnish:

Freshly grated Parmesan cheese

Chopped fresh parsley

Chopped fresh basil

Prep Time: 15 minutes
Cook Time: 2 hours 20 minutes
Yield: Serves 4

ALL-PURPOSE CHICKEN STOCK

The more whole chicken you butcher at home, the more your freezer will fill with bones and carcasses . . . until you have enough to make homemade chicken stock! One or two birds won't produce much, so you have to collect for a while—but the results will be worth the wait.

Homemade chicken stock is versatile and much more flavorful than what you'll find in a grocery store. I can't stress how much I love homemade chicken stock. This recipe is one I recommend trying immediately: Every dish you make with this chicken stock as the base will be a home run.

Instructions

1. Fill a large stockpot with the water. Place all of the chicken bones in the pot, then add the carrot, celery, onion, bay leaf, peppercorns, parsley, and garlic. Don't cover the stockpot or let the ingredients come to a boil—just bring them to a simmer.

2. Add the white wine vinegar, which helps to pull nutrients out of the bones.

3. Keep the stock barely simmering with minimal bubbling for 8 hours. Add more water as needed to keep the bones and vegetables completely submerged, usually a cup or two.

4. Skim the fat off the top as needed, but never stir the stock.

5. Line a colander with cheesecloth and place it over a large bowl. Strain the stock slowly through the colander, discarding any solids and scum at the bottom of the pot.

6. Let the stock cool at room temperature for at least an hour, then refrigerate overnight.

7. The next day, remove the solidified fat from the surface of the liquid.

8. Store the chicken stock in the refrigerator for 2 to 3 days, or in the freezer for up to 3 months. For ease of use, I like to store my stock in 2 to 4 cup measurements (0.6 to 1.135 L) in resealable freezer bags.

INGREDIENTS

2 gallons (7.6 L) water, plus a few extra cups

5 pounds (2.3 kg) raw chicken back, neck and wing bones

2 cups (256 g) roughly chopped carrot

2 cups (256 g) roughly chopped celery

2 cups (104 g) roughly chopped onion

1 bay leaf

1 teaspoon peppercorns

4 sprigs parsley

2 garlic cloves, smashed

1 tablespoon (15 ml) white wine vinegar

Prep Time: 15 minutes
Cook Time: 8 hours
Yield: 2 gallons (7.6 L)

Pork

PORK PRIMALS

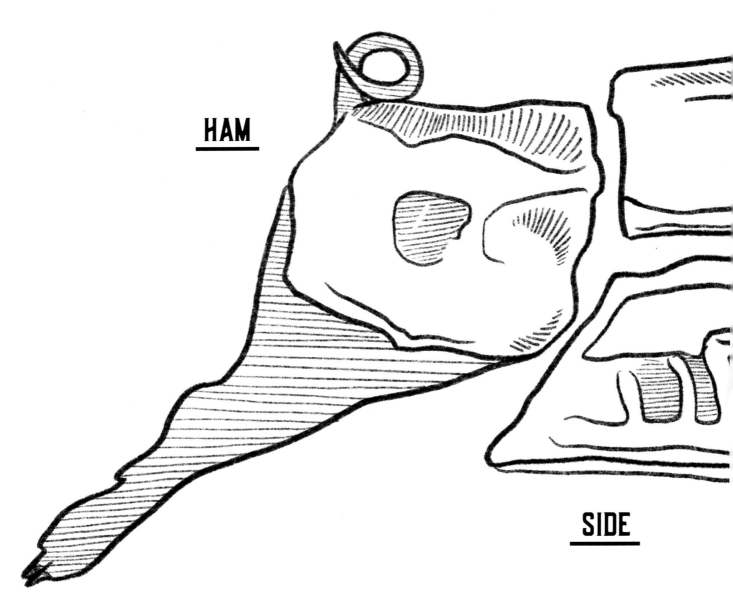

HAM

SIDE

LOIN

SHOULDER

PORK CUTS EXPLAINED

Pigs are not native to North America. Spanish explorers brought them in the sixteenth century. Within a hundred years, it was common for an average farmer to own a few pigs to supply their families with food and sell the remaining meat to their local communities.

In 1887, refrigerated railroad cars were introduced, which helped the commercial pork industry expand exponentially: Butchered meat could now be shipped to stores instead of shipping live hogs for slaughter and butchering near where their meat would be sold.

Today, many people are finding their way back to simpler times, butchering livestock themselves at home or buying meat from trusted butchers and farmers within their local communities.

PORK PRIMALS

The first step in the butchering process is to break the animal down into large, initial cuts of meat. As I described in the Butchery section on page 35, these primals are typically broken down further into smaller cuts, subprimals, which are individual cuts of meat that are a more manageable for cooking. The primals on a pig include the shoulder, loin, side, and leg.

There are many ways to break down a pig. The list here is not comprehensive, but rather a starting point for you to learn from and gain confidence in your exploration of new cuts of pork.

Shoulder

Alternate names: chuck, blade, front quarter

The front quarter of a pig, known as the shoulder primal, is made up of strong muscles, connective tissue, and fat. The muscle groups in the shoulder are used by the animal for movement, which makes these working muscles tough, dark, and flavorful. There are two subprimals found in the shoulder, the Boston butt and the picnic. The picnic subprimal is divided further into the picnic roast, hock, and front trotter.

Subprimals of the Shoulder

Boston butt. The Boston butt, also known as the blade shoulder or pork butt, comes from the top of the front shoulder. It's a tough cut of the meat that is best cooked at low temperatures for a long time. Particularly popular in the barbecue world for pulled pork, this cut has the right ratio of fat marbling to meat. The tough connective tissue and densely flavored meat breaks down into fall-apart tender pulled pork when cooked correctly and is my preferred cut from the front shoulder.

- This cut can be fabricated as a bone-in or boneless Boston butt.

- Cooking methods: braise, barbecue, grill roast, roast, slow roast, sous vide, stew

Country-style ribs. Meaty and flavorful, country-style ribs are cut from the upper side of the rib cage, from the blade end of the front shoulder. They are fatty and are made up of a mix of darker meat from the shoulder and lighter meat from the loin. Country-style ribs tend to be a less appreciated, though affordable, cut that has a lot of potential for creating droolworthy meals.

- Cooking methods: braise, stew, grill

Picnic roast. The picnic roast, also known as the arm shoulder, the pork shoulder, the picnic ham, or the arm roast, is frequently outshone by an adjacent cut, the Boston butt. Found in the bottom half of the shoulder, the picnic roast suffers from being tougher and less desirable, as are other cuts found lower on the animal. While the picnic roast still boasts a lot of flavor, it is an extremely tough cut, with complex, oddly shaped muscles and some unpleasant sinewy connective tissues. Nonetheless, slow-cooking methods can make it tender. Just below the picnic roast is the hock, which is a tough muscle that adds great flavor to stews, soups, and beans. And just below the hock is the pork foot, which is a primary ingredient in gelatin.

- This cut can be fabricated as a bone-in or boneless picnic roast.
- Cooking methods: braise, grill roast, roast, slow cook

Loin

The loin covers the main area of the animal's spine, containing all the delicious, tender muscles that surround the backbone. It runs from just behind the front shoulder to the top of the back leg. With its lean, tender meat, the loin is one of the most desirable primals on the animal. The entire loin can be roasted or cut into chops (that is, steaks cut from the loin).

Subprimals of the Loin

Pork chops. Not all pork chops are created equal. Where the pork chop is cut from the loin greatly affects its tenderness and flavor. Rib chops are cut from the rib section of the loin, so they have a little more fat and are some of the most flavorful chops from the loin. Chops cut from the center of the loin are lean and tender, but they can dry out easily due to their low fat content. Thicker bone-in chops tend to yield the juiciest results.

- Cooking methods: braise, grill, pan sear, roast

PRIMAL · PRIMAL · PRIMAL

Loin roasts. Similar to pork chops, you can cut a wide variety of roasts from the loin. These include blade-end roasts, center-cut rib roasts, center-cut pork loin roasts, and sirloin roasts. The closer to the shoulder you get, the tougher, but this meat will be more flavorful.

Blade-end rib roasts can be cut boneless or bone-in and are derived from the front of the pork loin near the blade shoulder.

The center of the loin is supremely tender, the location of some of the most expensive cuts of pork. Center-cut rib roasts, which are considered the prime rib of pork, are uniform in shape, mild, and fairly lean. The center-cut pork loin roast is always boneless, tender, has less fat than other roasts from the loin, and is extremely mild in flavor. The sirloin roast is cut from the end of the loin closest to the hindquarter of the pig—a flavorful cut, but tough.

- Cooking methods: braise, grill, roast

Tenderloin. The tenderloin is the most tender cut on the entire animal. It's shaped like a miniature boneless pork loin and is mildly flavored, with a low fat content. An excellent cut to roast in the oven because of its manageable size, it offers an even shape for a simple, yet tasty, meal. The tenderloin can be cut whole as its own cut of meat or cut with the loin to create a center-cut pork chop, also known as a porterhouse. This cut contains both the loin and the tenderloin in a single chop, divided by a bone running through the middle.

- Cooking methods: pan sear, roast, sous vide, stir-fry

Baby back ribs. Popular in the barbecue world, baby back ribs are cut from the section of the ribs closest to the loin, making them the most expensive ribs on a pig. They're leaner than other cuts of ribs, like the spareribs that are found near the belly, so beware of drying them out. Like all pork ribs, it's important to remove the thin membrane located on the inside of the ribs (covered below) prior to cooking.

- Cooking methods: barbecue, grill, roast

Leaf lard. The leaf lard offers some of the cleanest, least "porky"-tasting fat available on the pig. Derived from the soft fat around the pig's kidneys, leaf lard can be rendered into pure lard, perfect for sweet-and-savory cooking or baking.

Side

Alternate name: belly

The side primal is the moneymaker of a pig. It's where we get pork belly, one of the most beloved cuts from the whole animal. When salted and cured, pork belly becomes mouthwatering bacon. But another cut comes from the belly, equally treasured in the barbecue world: the meaty spareribs.

Subprimals of the Side

Spareribs. The spareribs come from the portion of the rib cage closest to the belly of the pig. They are a large, untrimmed section of the rib cage that contain the brisket bone and surrounding meat. A rack of spareribs can weigh over 5 pounds (2.3 kg). St. Louis–style ribs are a trimmed, clean-cut version of the spareribs, and they're more manageable in size, typically around 3 pounds (1.4 kg).

- Cooking methods: roast, barbecue

Pork belly. Uncured pork belly is the precursor to bacon. A boneless cut of meat found on the abdomen of the pig, it's loaded with fat and well marbled meat. Uncured pork belly is a staple in Asian and Latin cuisines.

- Cooking methods: braise, sous vide, roast

Leg

Alternate names: ham, round, hindquarter

The leg is best known for producing one of the most popular seasonal dishes of all time: holiday ham. Cured and smoked, these hams are distinctive with their beautiful pink flesh.

A fresh ham, on the other hand, is a raw cut of meat that has white flesh and tastes like a pork roast after cooking.

The leg of a pig is divided into two subprimals, the sirloin-end and shank-end fresh hams.

Subprimals of the Leg

Sirloin. The sirloin end of a fresh ham, sometimes called the butt ham, has a complex bone structure and is relatively lean but difficult to carve. Because of this, it's not as preferred for roasting as the shank-end fresh ham. I like to grind the sirloin and use the result for things like sausage, meatballs, and burgers. The sirloin can also be cut into steaks, although they are quite tough.

- Cooking methods: roasting, braising

Shank-end fresh ham. The shank-end fresh ham is a meaty, tapered cut of meat covered with a thick layer of fat. It's fattier and easier to carve than the sirloin-end fresh ham. This cut is great for slow roasting or braising in the oven.

- Cooking methods: roasting, braising

Secondary Cut

Ham hocks. The hock is a tough cut of meat, found just above the foot of the pig. It's full of fat and connective tissue with a little bit of meat surrounding the bone. In supermarkets, it's common to find presmoked and cured ham hocks. I like to keep my ham hocks fresh and raw, though, using them for a flavorful addition to beans and soups.

HOW TO BUTCHER A PIG

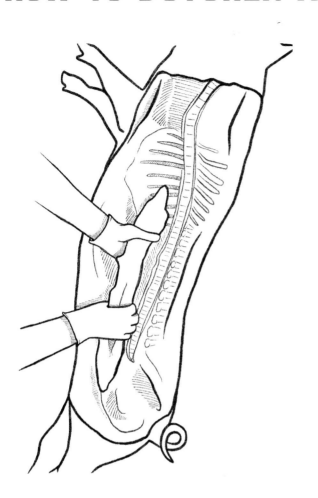 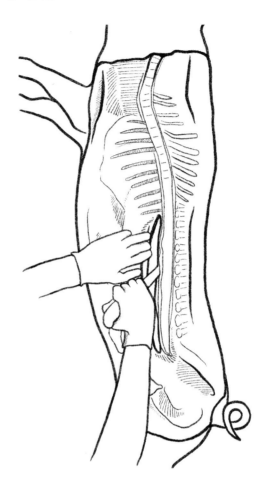

1. **Remove the leaf lard.** This is a large, rectangular mass of fat located on the inside cavity of the abdomen around the kidneys, with a portion of the fat next to the tenderloin. To remove, grab the top of the leaf lard and give it a firm, quick yank. The connective tissue will tear easily, allowing the fat to be removed with minimal knife cuts.

2. **Remove the tenderloin.** Locate the insertion point where the tenderloin connects to the leg muscles. Make a horizontal cut at the insertion point, then use the tip of the knife to continue tracing the upper edge of the tenderloin where it connects to the spine. Fillet the meat away from the bones in one solid piece.

3. **Remove the leg.** Start by separating the belly and the flank from the leg. Using your boning knife, make a cut where the thin, soft flank meets the firm, strong leg (see illustration 3a). Continue making a cut toward the loin until you reach the spine. Work your knife through the last two vertebrae of the loin to help loosen the connection. Starting from the top of the back, cut through the loin toward your previous knife cuts between the last two vertebrae. Using a bone saw or cleaver, complete the separation (see illustration 3b). Lift the leg and use leverage to split the spine, releasing the leg from the rest of the body.

4. **Remove the shoulder.** Count the first four ribs of the rib cage. The first rib can get lost under meat, so be careful to count correctly. Using your knife, make a long cut between the fourth and fifth ribs all the way down through the sternum. Continue this cut up toward the spine and score the connection between the fourth and fifth vertebrae. Starting from the top of the back, cut through the loin toward your previous knife cuts, between the fourth and fifth vertebrae. Use a saw to cut between the vertebrae, then continue to saw through the scapula (shoulder blade). If there is still meat within this cut, use a knife to slice through the meat and switch back to the bone saw until the shoulder is freed from the rest of the body.

5. **Remove the belly from the loin.** Make a mark with your knife on each end of the slab 2 to 3 inches (5 to 7.6 cm) from the loin eye. Using a knife, cut through the ribless section of the belly and continue to score through the ribs to connect the two marks. Using a saw, cut through the rib bones. Use a knife to cut through any remaining muscles.

Tips

- When deboning meat, use the curvature of the bone as your guide to fillet the meat off the bone. Keep your knife blade pointed toward the bone to minimize the amount of meat left on the bone. Any cut can be deboned; it's as simple as filleting the meat from the bone in one contiguous piece.

- Use a saw to cut through bone only. This means swapping back and forth between your knife and saw as needed during the butchering process. Once you break through the bone with your saw, change to the knife before cutting more; always switch back to your knife to complete cuts through meat.

- When separating joints, bend the joint back and forth to see where the bones come together. Make exploratory cuts with your knife and work through the ligaments and connective tissue that hold the joint together. Use leverage to pop joints and then continue cutting with your knife to finish the separation.

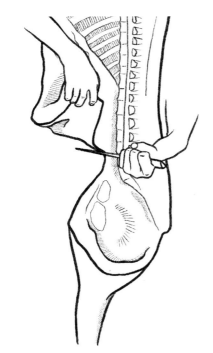

3a.

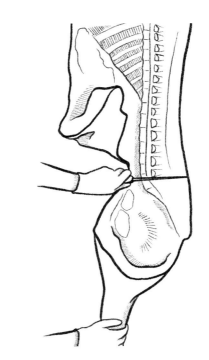

3b.

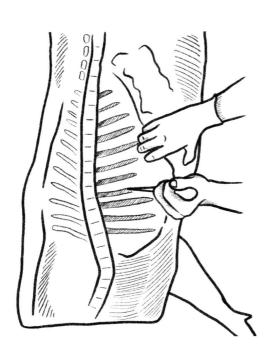

4.

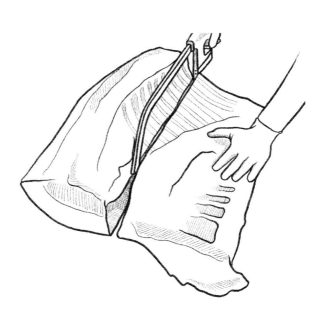

5.

Going Further

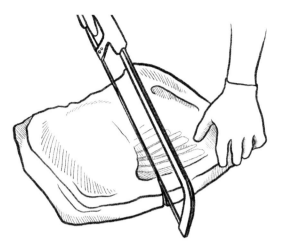

Separate the Boston butt from the picnic.

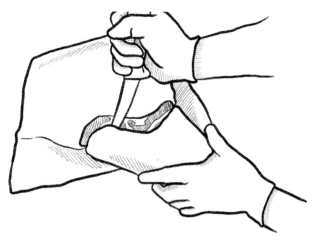

Remove the hock from the picnic.

Separate the Boston butt from the picnic.
Locate the connection between the first rib and the spine. Using a saw, cut through the connection point and continue that cut across all of the ribs. The cut will be parallel to the top of the shoulder. Switch back to a knife to cut through muscle until you hit the scapula. Saw through the scapula with your bone saw and then switch back to a knife to complete cutting through the muscles.

Remove the hock from the picnic. Cut through the joint and surrounding ligaments connecting the hock to the picnic. Using the edge of the table as leverage, break open the joint. Use a knife to cut through any remaining muscles until the hock is freed from the picnic.

Cut country-style ribs. Country-style ribs are a chineless shoulder chop cut in half lengthwise. They are cut from both the Boston butt and the rib end of the loin. To cut country-style ribs from the Boston butt, use a cimeter or large butcher

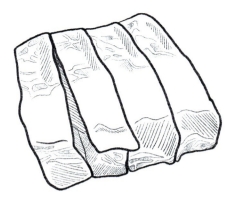

Cut country-style ribs.

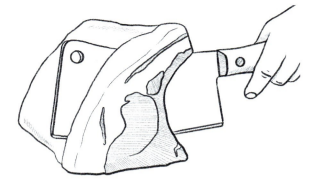

Cut bone-in chops..

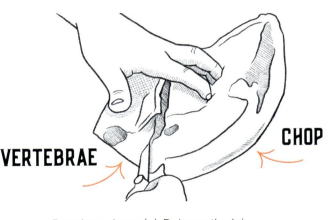

VERTEBRAE　　　**CHOP**

Boneless chops (a): Debone the loin.

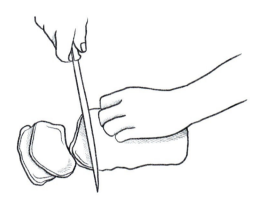

Boneless chops (b): Use a cimeter or
butcher knife to cut the loin into chops.

knife to slice through the rib-end section of
the meat until you hit the scapula. Use a saw
to cut through the bones of the scapula.
Continue cutting the meat into 1-inch (2.5-cm)
chops. Place each chop flat on the table and
slice through lengthwise for two even country-
style ribs.

Cut bone-in chops. With the fat side of the loin
facing up, use a cimeter or large butcher knife
to slice through the meat of the loin until you hit
the spine. Use a saw to cut through the bones
of the spine. Continue cutting chops of the
desired thickness from the loin.

Cut boneless chops. Follow the edge of the
finger bones with your knife blade until you hit
the spine. Work your knife around the ridge,
then, keeping your blade angled toward the
bone, continue filleting the feather bones away
from the meat (see illustration a). Place the loin
fat-side up and use a cimeter or large butcher
knife to cut the loin into chops of the desired
thickness (see illustration b).

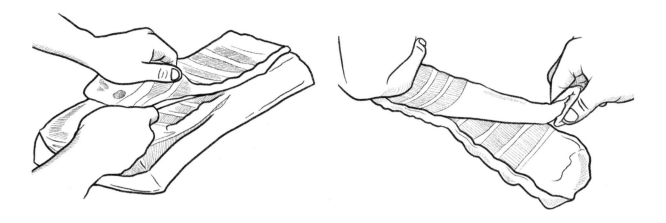

Cut baby back ribs.

Remove the rib membrane.

Cut baby back ribs. Using your free hand, pull the ribs as you use your knife to work one side of the rack away from the loin, staying close to the rib bones to keep as much meat as possible on the loin. Because the ribs are curved, it is easiest to fillet until you hit the center of the rack, then repeat the same process on the opposite edge. Work toward the center until the entire rack is freed from the loin.

Remove the rib membrane. At one end of the rack of ribs, slide a knife under the membrane to release it from the bone, meat, and fat. Lift the membrane to loosen it until it begins to tear away. Grab the edge of the membrane with a paper towel for extra grip and pull it off until all of the membrane is removed. Sometimes the membrane will come off in one whole piece; if it tears, you need to remove it in sections.

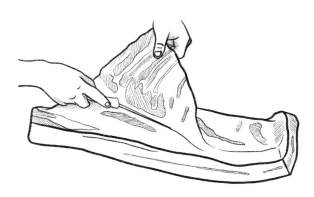

Spareribs: Using a boning knife, make a cut where the thin, soft flank meets the firm, strong leg.

St. Louis–style spareribs: Using a bone saw or cleaver, complete the separation.

Remove the spareribs from the belly. Starting at the shoulder end, use your knife to cut the underside of the ribs. Lift the ribs with your opposite hand and continue to cut until they are released from the belly.

Cut St. Louis–style spareribs. The bottom edge of the spareribs connect to the sternum via cartilage. Use a knife to score a line about 1 inch (2.5 cm) above the point where the ribs meet the cartilage. Use a saw to continue cutting through the bones. Square the end by using a knife to cut off the two smallest ribs at the end of the rack.

BONE-IN SMOKED AND SHREDDED BOSTON BUTT

The Boston butt is the most popular cut to use when making pulled pork, and for good reason: It's rich and succulent when cooked slowly. The name for this cut, however, is misleading. The Boston butt is from the top of the front shoulder, not from the butt of the pig.

A bone-in Boston butt smoked for a long time at low temperature will yield fall-apart-tender shreds of pork. Pair this with a toasted bun and a dollop of homemade barbecue sauce and you have the main course for a backyard cookout.

Instructions

1. Using a sharp boning knife, trim off the excess hard, waxy fat from the surface of the pork, leaving a ¼-inch (6-mm) layer in the fat cap that sits on the top of the roast. Next, cut slits in a cross-hatch pattern in the fat, about 1 inch (2.5 cm) apart, being careful not to cut all the way through to the meat.

2. Coat the entire cut of meat with olive oil, then use your hands to generously cover all of the meat with a ⅓ cup (69 g) of brown sugar pork rub. Press the rub into the meat to help it stick. To make things easier, use one hand to slather and turn the meat and the other to press in the rub. Flip and repeat on all sides.

3. Allow the pork to come to room temperature on the kitchen counter for an additional 20 minutes. This important step ensures even cooking and a juicer end product. It also allows time for the meat to absorb the rub and the salt to draw out the internal moisture.

4. Preheat the smoker to 275°F (135°C) using hickory pellets.

5. Cook the meat fat-cap up, unwrapped, until the internal tempera-ture reaches 165°F (74°C) and a richly colored bark forms on the outside of the meat. This will take 4 to 6 hours depending on the size of your Boston butt. Spray the meat with apple cider vinegar every 1 to 2 hours to keep it moist.

Continued

INGREDIENTS

1 6-to-8–pound (2.7 to 3.6–kg) bone-in Boston butt

2 tablespoons (30 ml) olive oil

⅓ cup (69 g) plus 1 tablespoon (15 g) brown sugar pork rub (page 96), divided

¼ cup (59 ml) apple cider vinegar

¼ cup (55 g) light brown sugar

¼ cup (54 g) unsalted butter, sliced into squares

1 cup (208 ml) homemade barbecue sauce (page 95)

1 tablespoon (14 g) unsalted butter per bun

Hamburger or brioche buns, for serving

Prep Time: 30 minutes
Cook Time: 6 to 9 hours
Yield: Serves 18 to 24

6. Remove the meat from the smoker and place it in a deep aluminum baking dish. Sprinkle with the remaining 1 tablespoon (15 g) of pork rub and the light brown sugar. Evenly space the pats of butter across the meat, then spray with more apple cider vinegar. Cover with aluminum foil.

7. Continue to smoke covered at 275°F (135°C) until the internal temperature reaches between 200°F and 205°F (93°C to 96°C). This will take an additional 2 to 3 hours.

8. Allow the meat to rest for at least 30 minutes.

9. Pour the pan juice into a fat separator, saving the juice to pour back onto the pork after it's shredded. Too much fat creates an oily mouthfeel, so it's important to remove the excess.

10. Shred the meat. I find it best to wear disposable gloves and shred the meat by hand, but you can also use two large, sturdy forks. First pull out the bone, which should fall away from the meat easily. Then use your fingers or forks to separate the meat into bite-sized pieces.

11. Pour the barbecue sauce onto the shredded pork (adjust the amount of sauce according to how you like your pulled pork). With your gloved hands, mix until the meat is evenly coated.

12. In a large skillet over medium heat, melt the butter. Place the buns in the pan cut-side down and toast until the buns are golden brown, about 30 seconds. Season with a small amount of kosher salt.

13. Serve the pork on the toasted buns with a dollop of homemade barbecue sauce.

HOMEMADE BARBECUE SAUCE

Barbecue sauce is easy to make at home, and it tastes much better than what you'll find in a grocery store. If I'm eating barbecue, this is the sauce I drown my plate in.

I love this recipe because of the freshly grated yellow onion, sweet apple juice, and bold pork rub that combine in this sauce for incredible depth of flavor. I keep this barbecue sauce stored in a squeeze bottle in my refrigerator.

Instructions

1. In a medium saucepan over medium heat, add the ketchup, brown sugar, lemon juice, butter, hot sauce, Worcestershire sauce, onion, brown sugar pork rub, and apple juice. Stir until combined.

2. Bring to a boil, then immediately reduce to a simmer over low heat until thickened, about 30 minutes.

3. Store in an airtight container in the refrigerator for up to 2 weeks.

INGREDIENTS

1 cup (24 g) ketchup (I recommend Heinz)

1 cup (150 g) light brown sugar

Juice from half of a lemon

3 tablespoons (45 g) unsalted butter

1 teaspoon hot sauce

1 teaspoon Worcestershire sauce

¼ of a yellow onion, finely grated

1 tablespoon (15 g) brown sugar pork rub (page 98)

½ cup (118 ml) apple juice

Prep Time: 5 minutes
Cook Time: 35 minutes
Yield: About 2 cups (475 ml)

BROWN SUGAR PORK RUB

This rub is magic. Its depth of flavors transforms pork into the perfect sweet, spicy, rich creation. Whether you're making pulled pork, baby back ribs, or even pork chops, this brown sugar rub is a must. It's a reliable rub that never disappoints.

This recipe makes enough rub to fit in a 12-ounce (355-ml) Mason jar. If you need more, it can easily be doubled; if you need less, cut it in half. However much you make, it'll taste just as great.

Instructions

1. In a large bowl, mix the brown sugar, kosher salt, black pepper, smoked paprika, chili powder, turmeric, garlic powder, onion powder, and cayenne pepper.

2. Break up any clumps, particularly in the brown sugar. I find it easiest to use my hands for this.

3. Store in an airtight jar and use on your favorite barbecue pork recipes.

Tip: Be sure to use smoked paprika in this recipe. I use Spice Islands Smoked Paprika. Buying the right paprika can make a huge difference in your rub's flavor, so pay attention while you're at the grocery store. It's also critical to use kosher salt and not table salt. If you try to substitute with table salt, the result will be unpleasantly salty.

INGREDIENTS

½ cup (110 g) packed light brown sugar

¼ cup (76 g) kosher salt (see Tip)

¼ cup (62 g) black pepper

2 tablespoons (14 g) smoked paprika (see Tip)

1½ tablespoons (11 g) chili powder

1½ tablespoons (9 g) turmeric

1½ teaspoons garlic powder

1½ teaspoons onion powder

1 teaspoon cayenne pepper

Prep Time: 5 minutes
Cook Time: 0 minutes
Yield: Just under 1½ cups (355 ml)

REVERSE SEARED PORK CHOPS WITH APPLE RELISH

This is one of my favorite ways to eat pork chops. The sweetness of the caramelized apples offsets the tanginess of the vinegar in the relish. Together they create the most delicious companion to juicy, seasoned-from-within pork chops. I love the subtle kiss of fresh sage and thyme that makes every bite of pork irresistible.

Instructions

1. In a large bowl, mix the apple cider, thyme, sage, and kosher salt.

2. Place the pork chops into the bowl, making sure they're completely covered with marinade. Cover and refrigerate for 2 to 4 hours.

3. Drain the liquid from the bowl and discard. Move the pork chops to a plate.

4. Allow the pork to come to room temperature on the kitchen counter for at least 30 minutes. This important step ensures even cooking and a juicer end product. While waiting, make two to three small slits in the fatty rind of each chop to prevent the meat from curling up in the skillet and ensure even searing. Dry the pork thoroughly with paper towels. Finally, season the pork chops with kosher salt and freshly ground black pepper.

5. Preheat the oven to 250°F (121°C). Prepare a baking sheet with a wire rack on top. Place the pork chops on the wire rack.

6. In a medium bowl, mix the rice vinegar, apple cider, sugar, and salt until dissolved. Add the apples, onion, and sweet red peppers. Mix, cover, and refrigerate until ready to serve.

7. Place the baking sheet with the pork chops in the preheated oven. Bake until they reach an internal temperature of 110°F (43°C), about 30 minutes.

Continued

INGREDIENTS

For the marinade:

3 cups (738 ml) apple cider

6 sprigs fresh thyme

2 fresh sage leaves

2 teaspoons kosher salt

For the pork:

4 center-cut loin pork chops (thickness: 1½ inches; 3.8 cm)

Kosher salt and freshly ground black pepper

2 tablespoons (30 ml) avocado oil

For the apple relish:

½ cup (117 ml) rice vinegar

¼ cup (58 ml) apple cider

½ cup (100 g) sugar

¼ teaspoon kosher salt

1 cup (140 g) peeled and finely chopped apples

½ large sweet onion, finely chopped

½ cup (26 g) finely chopped sweet red pepper

Continued

8. In a heavy, medium-sized skillet, melt the butter and sugar over medium-high heat. Add the apples and let them cook down until golden brown.

9. Remove the skillet from the heat. Stir in the lemon juice. Place the apples in a bowl for serving and set aside.

10. As the pork chops near 110°F (43°C), heat a large cast-iron skillet over medium-high heat. Add 2 tablespoons (30 ml) of oil and heat until the oil flows like water when the skillet is tilted.

11. Remove the pork chops from the oven and sear in batches, placing each chop in the hot skillet with a bit of space in between. You should hear sizzling from the moment the pork hits the pan. Sear each side of the pork chop for about 2 to 3 minutes, along with the fat cap, until a brown crust forms.

12. On a plate, place a pork chop on top of a bed of caramelized apples, then top with the apple relish and serve.

For the caramelized apples:

⅓ cup (72 g) unsalted butter

⅔ cup (147 g) brown sugar

4 Granny Smith apples, cored and thinly sliced

1 teaspoon fresh lemon juice

Prep Time: 15 minutes plus 2 to 4 hours marinating
Cook Time: 45 minutes
Yield: Serves 4

PICNIC CARNITAS

As we've seen, the picnic roast comes from the lower portion of the front shoulder of the pig, which means it's a tough but flavorful cut of meat. Unlocking its full potential requires extended cooking times at low temperature. The picnic roast is not uniformly shaped and unfolds in a way that makes it tricky to cook, which is why I recommend a bone-in cut that will hold together better or adding extra support by trussing it with kitchen twine.

The picnic roast is a more affordable cut that can be challenging to work with, but this carnitas recipe is a great way to make the most of it and transform the tough meat into tender shreds of flavorful pork.

Instructions

1. Trim the pork to remove excess fat, then salt liberally with kosher salt. Wrap tightly with plastic wrap and place in the refrigerator for 12 to 24 hours. Salt applied to the meat in advance makes a big difference in flavor and tenderness. (See page 22 for more information.)

2. About 30 minutes prior to cooking, remove the pork from the refrigerator and allow it to come to room temperature. This important step aids in even cooking.

3. In a small bowl, combine the 1 tablespoon (23 g) kosher salt, black pepper, garlic powder, onion powder, Mexican oregano, cumin, and coriander. Set aside.

4. Dry the pork shoulder thoroughly with paper towels.

5. Tie the pork with twine to make its shape as uniform as possible for even cooking. (See page 26 for information on how to tie a roast with twine).

6. Coat the entire cut of meat with 1 tablespoon of olive oil, then season generously all over with the rub. To make things easier, use one hand to slather and turn the meat and the other to press in the rub so it sticks to the meat. Flip and repeat on all sides.

Continued

INGREDIENTS

For the pork:

4 pound (1.8 kg) bone-in, skinless picnic roast

Kosher salt

For the rub:

1 tablespoon (23 g) kosher salt

1 tablespoon (6 g) freshly ground black pepper

1½ teaspoons garlic powder

1½ teaspoons onion powder

1 teaspoon Mexican oregano

Note: *It's worth looking for this ingredient if possible rather than substituting with conventional oregano.*

1 teaspoon ground cumin

½ teaspoon ground coriander

For the pork:

2 tablespoons (30 ml) olive oil, divided

1 onion, chopped

2 jalapeños, seeded and chopped

5 cloves garlic, minced

¾ cup (186 ml) freshly squeezed orange juice (2 oranges)

Feta cheese, for garnish

Freshly chopped cilantro, for garnish

Prep Time: 15 minutes plus 12 to 24 hours tenderizing

Cook Time: 8 to 10 hours

Yield: Serves 12

7. Place the pork in a slow cooker with the fat cap up. Add the onion, jalapeño, garlic, and orange juice. Cook on low for 8 to 10 hours.

8. Remove pork from the slow cooker and allow it to rest and cool for 30 minutes, with the twine still on. Keep everything else in the slow cooker and set aside.

9. Put on a pair of food-safe disposable gloves. Cut the twine with a pair of scissors and discard. Locate the bone within the meat and pull it out. Use your fingers or two sturdy forks to shred the pork into bite-sized pieces. After shredding, roughly chop the meat to shorten the muscle fibers.

10. Strain the juice from the slow cooker through a colander and into a fat separator. Discard the onions and jalapeños. Once separated, save the juice and set it aside for later. Too much fat creates an oily mouthfeel, so it's important to remove the excess.

11. Place a medium cast-iron skillet over high heat and add the remaining 1 tablespoon of oil. Spread a batch of pork in the skillet—be sure not to overcrowd the pan, or you will not achieve proper browning. Drizzle the meat with the reserved juice from the slow cooker. After the juices evaporate and the bottom of the pork begins to turn golden brown and crusty, flip the pork over and lightly sear the other side. The pork shouldn't be crispy on all sides, but rather it should yield some tender and juicy bites. Continue searing in batches.

12. Drizzle more juice over the pork immediately before serving. Garnish with freshly chopped cilantro and feta cheese.

SOY-GLAZED COUNTRY-STYLE RIBS WITH FRESH GINGER

For the longest time I didn't know that country-style ribs aren't actually ribs. I never put much thought into where they came from on a pig until I developed an interest for butchering.

As it turns out, country-style ribs aren't ribs at all: They're cut from the blade end of the loin of the pig, that is, the shoulder end of the loin. The meat is tough, which makes it a perfect choice for lower-temperature, longer-duration cooking. It's dark in color with lots of marbling and flavor.

I love the sweet heat of this recipe and the way the meat loses its toughness and transforms into tender bites after slow roasting in the oven.

Instructions

1. Salt the pork liberally with kosher salt. Cover and place in the refrigerator for 12 to 24 hours. Salt applied to the meat in advance makes a big difference in flavor and tenderness. (See page 22 for more information.)

2. About 30 minutes prior to cooking, remove the pork from the re-frigerator and allow it to come to room temperature. This important step ensures even cooking.

3. Preheat the oven to 350°F (177°C).

4. Dry the pork thoroughly with paper towels to aid in browning. Brush the pork with canola oil. Season with the 1 tablespoon (23 g) of kosher salt and light brown sugar.

5. Set a large oven-safe pan over medium heat. Add 1 tablespoon (30 ml) of oil and heat until it flows like water when the pan is tilt-ed. Place the pork into the pan to brown. The pork should sizzle when you place it in the pan. If it doesn't sizzle, your oil is not hot enough. Brown the pork evenly on all sides, about 2 to 3 minutes per side. Remove the browned meat from the pan and set aside.

Continued

INGREDIENTS

For the pork:

2 to 3 pounds (0.9 to 1.4 kg) country-style ribs

1 tablespoon (23 g) kosher salt, plus more for tenderizing

3 tablespoons (45 ml) canola oil, divided

2 tablespoons (30 g) light brown sugar

1 medium sweet onion, sliced

For the sauce:

½ cup (163 g) honey

½ cup (110 g) dark brown sugar

¼ cup (64 ml) reduced-sodium soy sauce

1 tablespoon (30 g) sriracha

2 teaspoons grated fresh ginger

1 teaspoon grated fresh garlic

½ cup (118 ml) water

1½ tablespoons (20 g) unsalted butter

4 whole dried chili peppers

Prep Time: 15 minutes plus 12 to 24 hours tenderizing
Cook Time: 1 hour 30 minutes
Yield: Serves 4

6. Remove as much of the fat from the pan as you can, then return the pan to the stove. Reduce the heat to medium low and add 1 more tablespoon (30 ml) of oil.

7. Add the onions and cook, stirring frequently, until they're tender and lightly browned, about 15 minutes.

8. In a medium bowl, combine the honey, brown sugar, soy sauce, sriracha, ginger, and garlic.

9. Add the water to the pan and, using a wooden spoon, scrape up any browned bits from the bottom of the pan. Place the pork back in the pan, on top of the onions, then pour the sauce all over the pork. The liquid should come about one-third to halfway up the pork.

10. Add the butter and dried chilies to the pan and bring to a boil.

11. Place the pan, uncovered, in the oven for about 1 hour, flipping once to cook evenly on both sides.

12. After the pork is fully cooked, place the pan back on the stovetop over medium heat and reduce the liquid to a sticky glaze, about 3 to 5 minutes.

SOUS-VIDE PORK TENDERLOIN WITH PEACH CHUTNEY

Pork tenderloin is one of the most tender cuts of meat on a pig. It is low in fat content and has a pleasantly mild flavor. A pork tenderloin is the perfect cut to dress up with bold flavors like this bright peach chutney.

There's more to love about a pork tenderloin: Naturally uniform in shape, the cuts will cook evenly without extra effort and are elegant enough to serve as the main dish for a special dinner.

Instructions

1. Salt the pork tenderloin liberally with kosher salt. Wrap tightly with plastic wrap and place in the refrigerator for 12 to 24 hours. Salt applied to the meat in advance makes a big difference in flavor and tenderness. (See page 22 for more information.)

2. Thirty minutes prior to cooking, remove the meat from the refrigerator and allow it to come to room temperature. This important step ensures even cooking.

3. Trim the meat, including the excess fat and silver skin (the opaque white membrane attached to the meat's surface).

4. Prepare a sous-vide water bath. For a medium-rare pork tenderloin (which will come out juicy with a light pink center), set the sous vide to 140°F (60°C). If you prefer your pork prepared medium, set the sous vide to 150°F (71°C).

5. Pat the meat dry with paper towels, then season it liberally with kosher salt and freshly ground black pepper. Press the seasoning into the meat on all sides. Place the pork and thyme in a bag and seal using a vacuum sealer (see sidebar on page 109).

6. Submerge the bag in the water bath and use a binder clip to secure the top of the bag to the rim of the container. This will keep the bag from floating to the surface. The meat should be fully submerged in the container. Cook for 1 hour.

Continued

INGREDIENTS

For the pork:

1 (1-pound/455 g) pork tenderloin

Kosher salt and freshly ground black pepper

5 fresh thyme sprigs

For the peach chutney:

3 ripe peaches, peeled and finely chopped

¾ cup (165 g) light brown sugar

½ cup (123 ml) apple cider vinegar

1 tablespoon (6 g) fresh ginger, minced

½ medium red onion, finely chopped

4 whole dried chilies, stemmed

Pinch of ground cloves

Kosher salt

2 tablespoons (30 ml) avocado oil

Prep Time: 10 minutes plus 12 to 24 hours tenderizing

Cook Time: 90 minutes

Yield: Serves 4

How to Seal It

If you don't have a vacuum sealer, you can still sous vide using the displacement method with a resealable plastic bag (I recommend a thicker freezer-style bag). To do this, press and seal all but one corner of the bag, then slowly lower your bagged meat or vegetables into a pot of water, letting the air release through the bag opening. Press to seal the remainder of the bag. The bag should be completely free of air and tightly sealed: Water shouldn't be able to enter the bag during the cooking process.

7. As you wait, make the peach chutney. First, bring a large pot of water to a boil. Fill a large bowl with ice water and set aside. With a paring knife, score the bottom of each peach.

8. Once the water is boiling, add the peaches to the water for just 30 seconds, then transfer them immediately into the ice water. When cool enough to handle, peel the peaches and cut them into small cubes.

9. In a medium-sized saucepan over medium-low heat, combine the brown sugar, apple cider vinegar, ginger, onion, chilies, and cloves. Simmer until the onions are soft, about 10 minutes.

10. Add the peaches and a pinch of kosher salt to the brown sugar mixture. Continue simmering over low heat until the peaches are soft and the entire mixture thickens and darkens a bit, about 45 minutes.

11. Carefully remove the sous-vide bag from the water bath. Take the pork out of the bag, discarding the thyme. Pat the pork dry with paper towels: This will create a good sear.

12. Place a large cast-iron pan over medium-high heat. Add the oil to the hot pan and heat until it flows like water when the pan is tilted. Place the pork in the pan; you should hear sizzling the moment the pork hits the oil. Sear the pork for 1 to 2 minutes on all sides until a brown crust forms.

13. Allow the pork to rest for 10 minutes, then top with peach chutney and serve.

STICKY-AND-SWEET BABY BACK RIBS

The 3:2:1 method is by far the best way to prepare pork ribs on the smoker if you like meat that falls off the bone. It's how I've always cooked them with my dad: Each time they turn out tender and delicious.

Cook the ribs for 3 hours uncovered, 2 hours wrapped in aluminum foil, and 1 final hour uncovered. While some smokers swear by their rigs, I love the simplicity of a pellet grill. I can set my desired temperature and the grill does the rest. And this method still yields the flavorful bark that forms through the cooking process.

Instructions

1. Remove the thin, tough membrane that covers the entire bone side of the ribs. Scoring the membrane first can help. Removing this membrane (see page 91) ensures a pleasant eating experience and will enable the rub to fully penetrate the meat.

2. Brush one side of the ribs with yellow mustard, then season generously with the brown sugar pork rub. Press the rub into the meat with your hands to help it stick. To make things easier, use one hand to slather and turn the meat and the other to sprinkle the rub and rub it in so it sticks. Flip and repeat on the opposite side. You'll use about ¼ cup (52 g) of the rub on the entire rack of ribs.

3. Allow the pork to come to room temperature on the kitchen counter for an additional 20 minutes. This important step ensures even cooking and a juicer end product. It also allows time for the meat to absorb the rub and the salt to draw out the internal moisture.

4. Preheat the smoker to 225°F (107°C) using hickory pellets.

5. Cook the ribs meat-side up, unwrapped, for 3 hours. Spray with apple cider every hour.

Continued

INGREDIENTS

1 rack baby back ribs

¼ cup (54 g) yellow mustard

¼ cup (52 g) plus 2 tablespoons (30 g) brown sugar pork rub (page 96), divided

½ cup (123 ml) apple cider, in a spray bottle

¼ cup (55 g) brown sugar, divided

3 tablespoons (45 g) unsalted butter, sliced into squares

2 cups (475 ml) homemade barbecue sauce (page 95), plus more for serving

---

Prep Time: 30 minutes
Cook Time: 6 hours
Yield: Serves 2 to 3

6. Measure out 2 pieces of aluminum foil that are twice the length of your rack of ribs. Set one aside. On the second, sprinkle 2 tablespoons (30 g) brown sugar and 1 tablespoon (15 g) pork rub, then spray with apple cider.

7. Remove the ribs from the smoker and place them meat-side down on the piece of aluminum foil you prepared with brown sugar, rub, and apple cider.

8. The bone side of the ribs creates a perfect vessel to hold more flavor. Sprinkle the top with 2 more tablespoons (30 g) brown sugar and 1 tablespoon (15 g) pork rub. Evenly space the pats of butter across the ribs, then spray with more apple cider. Wrap in the foil.

9. Wrap the ribs with the remaining sheet of aluminum foil. Double-wrapping provides extra durability to prevent the aluminum foil from tearing when taking the ribs on and off the grill. If the foil tears, you'll lose all the flavorful juices inside it.

10. Place the wrapped ribs back in the smoker, meat-side down, and cook for 2 hours.

11. Remove the ribs from the smoker, discard the aluminum foil, and brush with barbecue sauce. Place back in the smoker, uncovered with the meat-side up, for about 1 hour, or until the ribs reach an internal temperature of 200°F (93°C), or when the meat begins to recede from the bone.

12. Remove the cooked ribs from the grill and allow them to rest for 10 to 15 minutes before serving.

OVEN-ROASTED CENTER-CUT PORK LOIN WITH HERB SAUCE

A center-cut pork loin roast is tender, juicy, and evenly shaped for seamless cooking. Because this cut is so lean, I like to brine it before cooking to create an extremely moist end product.

The spice rub is filled with garlic, onion, and paprika. It adds a well-balanced flavor to complement the pork loin, which is a wonderful blank canvas. The herb sauce is simple and bright, adding a lovely fresh element to this dish.

I like to use russet potatoes for this recipe, but you can switch it up any number of ways, from sweet potatoes to Brussels sprouts or even butternut squash.

Instructions

1. In at least a 2-quart (1.8 L) pot, bring 1 quart (900 ml) of water, the sugar, and the kosher salt to a boil until everything is dissolved. Remove from heat and add 1 quart (900 ml) of cold water. Allow the brine to cool to room temperature.

2. *This is important:* Do not put the meat in the brine until it has cooled completely or else the hot water will begin to cook the meat.

3. Once the brine has cooled, place the pork loin in a large, deep container, like a roasting dish. Pour the brine over the meat, ensuring that it is completely covered by liquid. Cover and place in the refrigerator for 12 to 24 hours.

4. Thirty minutes to 1 hour prior to cooking, remove the pork from the brine and set it on a clean dish. Discard the brining liquid. Allow the meat to come to room temperature on the countertop. This important step helps it cook more evenly.

5. Adjust the oven rack to a lower-middle position and preheat the oven to 400°F (204°C).

6. In a large bowl, toss the potatoes with 1 tablespoon (15 ml) of olive oil, kosher salt, and black pepper. Spread the potatoes evenly onto a large roasting pan. Place a wire rack over the potatoes.

Continued

INGREDIENTS

For the brine:

2 quarts (1.9 L) water, divided

½ cup (144 g) kosher salt

¼ cup (50 g) granulated sugar

For the pork:

1 (3-pound/1.4-kg) boneless center-cut pork loin roast, tied at 1½-inch (3.8-inch) intervals

1 pound (455 g) russet potatoes, cubed

2 tablespoons (30 ml) olive oil, divided

Kosher salt and freshly ground pepper to taste

1 sprig fresh thyme

1 sprig fresh rosemary

For the spice rub:

1 tablespoon (7 g) paprika

1 tablespoon (9 g) garlic powder

1½ teaspoons onion powder

1½ teaspoons freshly ground black pepper

¼ teaspoon kosher salt

Continued

7. Pat the pork loin very dry with paper towels. Tie with twine to make its shape as uniform as possible for even cooking. (See page 26 for information on how to tie a roast with twine.)

8. In a small bowl, combine the paprika, garlic powder, and onion powder. Drizzle the pork loin with the remaining 1 tablespoon (15 ml) of olive oil and sprinkle the spice rub all over, patting it into the meat with your hands.

9. Place the pork roast on the wire rack fat-side up. The fat layer will melt and baste the meat as it cooks, which helps the pork stay moist. Roast the pork for 10 minutes at 400°F (204°C) to create a crust on the meat and seal in the flavorful juices.

10. Turn down the oven temperature to 350°F (177°C) and continue to cook the pork until it reaches an internal temperature of 140°F (60°C), between 50 minutes and 1 hour 15 minutes, depending on the thickness and size of the roast.

11. While the pork is roasting, combine the shallot and the vinegar in a small bowl. Set aside for 15 minutes until the onions are softened by the vinegar.

12. In a food processor, pulse the cilantro, olive oil, garlic, and sugar until the cilantro is finely chopped. Scrape down the sides of the food processor as needed.

13. Remove the roasting pan from the oven and transfer the pork loin to a carving board to rest for 20 minutes.

14. Increase the oven temperature to 450°F (232°C). Give the potatoes a stir and continue to roast until they are golden brown, about 10 minutes.

15. Remove the twine from the roast and slice.

16. Add the shallots and only 1 teaspoon of the vinegar to the herb sauce. Discard the remaining vinegar. Season with kosher salt and freshly ground black pepper to taste.

17. Serve the sliced pork with potatoes and herb sauce.

For the herb sauce:

½ shallot, grated

2 tablespoons (30 ml) white wine vinegar

2½ cups (928 g) fresh cilantro, including stems

½ cup (109 ml) extra virgin olive oil

2 garlic cloves

½ teaspoon white sugar

Kosher salt and freshly ground pepper to taste

Prep Time: 15 minutes plus 12 to 24 hours brining
Cook Time: 2 hours 30 minutes
Yield: Serves 3 to 5

GARLIC BUTTER BONELESS PORK CHOPS

I get it—pork chops have a reputation of being dry, bland, and boring. Certainly, I felt that way growing up. I used to scoff at my mom for making pork chops, but as my taste buds bloomed, I discovered how delightful they could be. This recipe is a perfect example of how to elevate a boring old pork chop. The simple breading enhances the texture of the dish while the creamy and indulgent sauce brings in flavors of Parmesan cheese and fragrant fresh thyme.

Instructions

1. Salt the pork liberally with kosher salt. Cover and place in the refrigerator for 12 to 24 hours. Salt applied to the meat in advance makes a big difference in flavor and tenderness. (See page 22 for more information.)

2. About 30 minutes prior to cooking, remove the pork from the refrigerator and allow it to come to room temperature. This important step ensures even cooking.

3. Make two to three small slits through the fatty rind of each chop to prevent the chops from curling up in the skillet and to ensure even searing. Dry the pork thoroughly with paper towels.

4. In a large bowl, whisk together the egg, cornstarch, salt, and pepper until well combined.

5. Add the pork to the bowl and mix with your hands until the pork is well coated on all sides.

6. Place a large cast-iron pan over medium high heat. Add the oil to the hot pan and heat until it flows like water when the pan is tilted. Place the pork chops into the hot pan. You should hear sizzling the moment the pork hits the oil. Sear the chops until a brown crust begins to form, about 3 to 4 minutes per side. Remove the chops from the pan and set them aside.

7. Pour out any excess fat from the pan, then lower the heat to medium. Melt the butter, then add the garlic and thyme. Cook for 1 minute until fragrant.

INGREDIENTS

2 boneless center-cut pork chops

1 teaspoon kosher salt, plus more for tenderizing

1 teaspoon freshly ground black pepper

1 egg

2 tablespoons (16 g) cornstarch

2 tablespoons (30 ml) avocado oil

1 tablespoon (14 g) unsalted butter

3 cloves fresh garlic, thinly sliced

3 sprigs thyme

1½ cups (353 ml) heavy cream

¼ cup (90 g) freshly grated Parmesan cheese

Fresh parsley for garnish

Meyer lemon slices for serving

Prep Time: 15 minutes plus 12 to 24 hours tenderizing
Cook Time: 20 minutes
Yield: Serves 2

8. Pour in the cream and, using a wooden spoon, scrape up any browned bits from the bottom of the pan.

9. Bring the mixture to a boil, then immediately reduce heat to low and put the pork back in the pan. Simmer for about 5 minutes while basting the meat with the sauce.

10. Once the internal temperature of the pork reaches 145°F (63°C), turn off the heat and stir in the Parmesan cheese until it melts, about 1 minute.

11. Remove the pan from the heat and allow the meat to rest for 5 to 10 minutes.

12. Plate the pork garnished with fresh parsley and lemon wedges.

OVEN BAKED HOT HONEY ST. LOUIS–STYLE SPARERIBS

St. Louis–style ribs are a more manageable version of spareribs that are trimmed to produce a narrow rack that weighs around 3 pounds (1.4 kg). St. Louis–style ribs are not as lean as baby back ribs, so they don't dry out as quickly and cook more consistently.

This recipe is designed for those who want ribs at home without the smoker. There is no replicating true smoky flavor (so if you have a smoker, use it), but with this recipe it's possible to create tender, juicy ribs in your home oven.

Instructions

1. Remove the membrane from the bone side of the ribs (see page 91). Scoring the membrane first can help, then use a paper towel to peel it off. Removing this membrane ensures a pleasant eating experience and will enable the rub to fully penetrate the meat.

2. Trim any excess fat away to create an even, clean surface for the rub to adhere to.

3. Brush one side of the ribs with olive oil, then season generously with brown sugar pork rub. To make things easier, use one hand to slather and turn the meat and the other to press in the rub to help it stick. Flip and repeat on the opposite side. You'll use roughly ¼ cup (52 g) of rub to season the entire rack of ribs.

4. Allow the pork to come to room temperature on the kitchen counter for an additional 20 minutes. This important step ensures even cooking and a juicer end product. It also allows time for the meat to absorb the rub and the salt to draw out the internal moisture.

5. Preheat the oven to 275°F (135°C). Prepare a baking sheet with a wire rack on top.

6. Place the ribs on the wire rack, meat-side up. Cook until a rich bark forms on the outside of the meat, about 2 hours. Spray with apple cider vinegar every 1 hour.

Continued

INGREDIENTS

1 rack St. Louis–style spareribs

2 tablespoons (30 ml) olive oil

¼ cup (52 g) plus 1 tablespoon (15 g) brown sugar pork rub (page 96), divided

¼ cup (55 g) brown sugar, divided

½ cup (123 ml) apple cider vinegar, in a spray bottle

3 tablespoons (45 g) unsalted butter, cut into squares

¼ cup (82 g) honey

½ cup (286 ml) homemade barbecue sauce (page 95), plus more for serving

1 tablespoon (20 g) hot sauce

1 dash liquid smoke

Prep Time: 30 minutes
Cook Time: 6 hours
Yield: Serves 2 to 3

7. Measure out 2 pieces of aluminum foil that are twice the length of your rack of ribs. Set one aside. On the second, sprinkle 2 tablespoons (30 g) brown sugar and spray it with apple cider vinegar.

8. Once the bark has formed on the ribs, remove them from the oven and place them meat-side down on top of the sheet of aluminum foil prepared with brown sugar.

9. The bone side of the ribs creates a perfect vessel to hold more flavor. Sprinkle the top with 2 more tablespoons (30 g) brown sugar and 1 tablespoon (15 g) pork rub. Place the pats of butter evenly across the ribs and then spray with more apple cider vinegar. Wrap the foil.

10. Wrap the foil around the ribs and then wrap them again with the remaining sheet of aluminum foil. Double-wrapping provides extra durability to prevent the aluminum foil from tearing when taking the ribs in and out of the oven. If the foil tears, you'll lose all of the flavorful juices inside it.

11. Place the wrapped ribs with the meat side down back in the oven and cook until they reach an internal temperature of 200°F (93°C), or when the meat begins to recede from the bone, about 2 hours.

12. While the ribs are cooking, combine the homemade barbecue sauce, honey, and hot sauce in a small bowl. Add only a dash of liquid smoke; do not overuse this flavoring, as it will dominate the dish if you add too much. Set aside.

13. Remove the cooked ribs from the oven and preheat the oven to 275°F (135°C).

14. Brush the ribs with the hot honey glaze, then place them back on the wired rack, meat-side up. Bake for about 10 minutes.

15. Allow the ribs to rest for 10 to 15 minutes before serving.

PEPPERED SMOKED BACON

Bacon is one of the greatest culinary discoveries of all time. Beautifully balanced, with velvety fat and rich, meaty flavor—and just enough salt to make your mouth water—it's also easy to make at home with a couple key pieces of equipment. You'll need a food scale, a smoker, and Prague powder #1 (see more about curing salts on page 33). The result is a succulent dish so fresh you'll never want store-bought bacon again.

Instructions

1. Using a kitchen scale, weigh your pork belly. Take the weight of the pork belly in grams and multiply by 0.0025; this gives you the weight in grams of Prague powder #1 needed.

2. Accuracy is critical when weighing and measuring Prague powder #1 because it is toxic to humans at high doses. Add the measured Prague powder #1 to a medium bowl.

> **Example:**
> Pork belly weighs 2,268 grams (5 pounds; 2.3 kg)
> 2268 x 0.0025 = 5.67 grams of Prague powder #1
> (about 1 ½ teaspoons)

3. Add the kosher salt, brown sugar, 3 tablespoons (18 g) black pepper, and the maple syrup to the bowl with the Prague powder #1. Mix until well combined.

4. Place the pork belly in a large plastic bag. With gloved hands, evenly coat the pork belly with the spice mixture. Make sure all of the spice mixture makes it onto the meat. This is important because we measured a specific amount of curing salt and it all needs to make it on the meat for it to cure properly.

5. Place the meat into the refrigerator for 7 to 10 days, flipping and massaging the spice rub into the meat once per day.

6. After 7 to 10 days, the outside of the pork belly will look deeper in color and dry, which is the sign that the cure worked. It should feel firm to the touch.

Continued

INGREDIENTS

5 pounds (2.3 kg) pork belly, skin off

1½ teaspoons Prague powder #1

¼ cup (76 g) kosher salt

¼ cup (55 g) packed dark brown sugar

6 tablespoons (36 g) ground black pepper, divided

¼ cup (80 g) maple syrup

Prep Time: 15 minutes plus 7- to 10-day cure

Cook Time: 3 to 4 hours

Yield: 3½ pounds (1.6 kg) of bacon

7. Prepare a rimmed stainless-steel baking sheet with a stainless-steel wire rack on top. If you don't have a stainless-steel baking sheet, opt for a glass dish instead, as other types of metal can react with the salt, causing off flavors. The wire rack is important for air circulation throughout the dry brining process and keeps the meat from coming into contact with liquid as it sits in the fridge.

8. Lightly rinse the pork belly, then pat dry with paper towels and season all sides liberally with freshly cracked pepper (approximately 3 tablespoons [18 g]), pressing it into meat with your hands.

9. Place the meat onto the prepared wire rack. Place back in the refrigerator, uncovered, for 24 hours. This will help dry out the surface of the meat and prepare it for the smoking process.

10. Preheat a smoker to 185°F (85°C).

11. Remove the meat from the fridge and place it on the smoker. Smoke the meat until it reaches an internal temperature of 152°F (67°C), about 3 to 4 hours.

12. Place the smoked bacon on a clean wire baking rack and allow it to cool. Once cooled, place the meat into your refrigerator to rest overnight.

13. After the meat is rested and cooled, it's time to slice. Using a meat slicer, slice the bacon to the desired thickness. If you don't have a slicer, you can cut by hand using a long, sharp knife like a cimeter or butcher's knife. If you like thinly sliced bacon, go for the slicer; it will be difficult to slice thin strips of bacon evenly with a knife.

14. Wrap the bacon slices in plastic wrap or vacuum seal them to keep fresh in the refrigerator for up to 2 weeks. To freeze the bacon, lay the bacon slices on a sheet of wax paper and place in a freezer-safe plastic bag or vacuum seal. I find vacuum sealing to be the best method for preserving freshness.

FRESH SHANK-END HAM WITH MOLASSES GLAZE

Fresh ham comes from the hindquarter of the pig. There are two primary cuts that break down from whole fresh ham: The sirloin section and the shank-end section. The sirloin is located toward the hip of the pig, while the shank end is the bottom half of the hindquarter. I prefer using the shank-end cut for this recipe because it is easier to carve than the sirloin section of the ham.

Brining the meat ahead of time infuses moisture and the fresh flavors of rosemary and thyme deep into the meat. The molasses glaze creates an irresistibly sweet blanket of flavor on the crust of the ham.

Instructions

1. Using a sharp boning knife, remove the skin from the ham. Be careful not to cut away too much of the fat. You want to keep about ¼ to ½ inch (6 mm to 1 cm) of fat on the meat.

2. With a very sharp knife, score the fat cap of the ham in a cross-hatch pattern. Cut about two-thirds of the way into the fat, without cutting into the meat of the ham.

3. In a large stockpot, boil 2 quarts (1.9 L) of water, the sugar, the rosemary, the thyme, the cloves, and the kosher salt. Cook for a few minutes until the sugar and salt have dissolved. Remove from the heat and add the remaining 2 quarts (1.9 L) of cold water. Allow the brine to cool to room temperature. *Important:* Do not move on to the next step until the brine has cooled completely.

4. Once the brine has cooled, skim out the rosemary, thyme, and cloves. Use a meat injector to inject the liquid brine into the pork. Push the needle into the meat at a 45-degree angle, going about 3 inches (7.6 cm) deep. Push the injector to expel the liquid as you pull the needle out. Leave about 2 inches (5 cm) of space between injections. Be thorough and inject the brine evenly throughout the ham. The muscles will swell as they're injected. You'll use approximately 3 cups (745 ml) of liquid.

INGREDIENTS

1 shank-end bone-in ham

For the brine:

4 quarts (3.8 liters) water, divided

½ cup (110 g) light brown sugar

2 sprigs fresh rosemary

2 fresh thyme sprigs

2 whole cloves

1 cup (288 g) kosher salt

For roasting:

⅓ cup (73 g) light brown sugar

⅓ cup (118 g) kosher salt

2 tablespoons (22 g) Dijon mustard

1 cup (251 ml) lager beer

1 cup (248 ml) apple juice

2 whole cloves

2 fresh thyme sprigs

For the glaze:

¼ cup (84 ml) molasses

¼ cup (80 g) maple syrup

2 teaspoons soy sauce

2 teaspoons Dijon mustard

1 tablespoon black pepper

Prep Time: 30 minutes plus 12 to 24 hours brining

Cook Time: 4 to 6 hours

Yield: Serves 8 to 10

Continued

5. Place the ham in a deep roasting dish and pour the remaining brine on top, ensuring that the meat is completely covered by liquid. Cover and place in the refrigerator for 12 to 24 hours.

6. One hour prior to cooking, remove the ham from the refrigerator. Take the ham out of the brine and set it on a clean dish. Pat very dry with paper towels and allow it to come to room temperature on the countertop. This important step helps the meat cook more evenly.

7. Truss the pork with twine to make its shape as uniform as possible for even cooking. (See page 48 for information on how to truss.)

8. Preheat the oven to 325°F (163°C). Prepare a roasting pan with a rack inside.

9. In a small bowl, mix together the brown sugar and kosher salt. Set aside.

10. Rub the ham all over with Dijon mustard, then rub the spice mixture over that. The mustard helps the rub stick to the meat.

11. Set the ham on the roasting rack, fat-side up. Add the beer, apple juice, cloves, and thyme.

12. Place the roasting pan in the oven and roast for 3½ to 5 hours, basting the ham every 30 minutes with the pan juices. If the top browns too quickly, loosely cover just those parts with aluminum foil. The roast is done when it reaches an internal temperature of 155°F (68°C) and the meat recedes cleanly from the bone.

13. While the meat is roasting, mix together the molasses, maple syrup, soy sauce, Dijon mustard, and black pepper in a medium bowl until well combined.

14. Once cooked, remove the roast from the oven and increase the oven temperature to 450°F (232°C). Brush the ham all over with the glaze and return it to the oven, uncovered, for 10 minutes to brown the outside of the meat.

15. Remove the ham from the oven and set it on a carving board. Loosely cover it with aluminum foil and allow it to rest for 30 to 40 minutes.

16. Pour the liquids from the pan into a fat separator. Allow it to set for 10 minutes, then remove the fat from the juices.

17. Carve the ham and serve with pan juices drizzled on top.

ITALIAN PORK SAUSAGE

I reach for fresh herbs whenever possible. When it comes to sausage making, though, dried herbs are a better because they're tougher.

Sausage making is an art, a tradition passed down from generation to generation. I made sausage for the first time with my Pap Pap, a stubborn Italian man who was born and raised in the rolling countryside of central Italy. We made venison sausage from a deer I harvested in Pennsylvania using a historic-looking, commercial-grade grinder and mixer he kept in his basement kitchen next to his meat cellar.

This is a great recipe to make in bulk when you have extra time, then freeze for future enjoyment. It's a variation on the one I learned from my late Pap Pap.

INGREDIENTS

1 teaspoon whole peppercorns

2 teaspoons fennel seeds

1 teaspoon anise seeds

2 pounds (900 g) ground pork

1½ teaspoons kosher salt

½ teaspoon white sugar

½ teaspoon dried oregano

½ teaspoon dried basil

¼ cup (60 ml) cold dry white wine

Prep Time: 10 minutes
Cook Time: 0 minutes
Yield: Serves 4 to 6

Instructions

1. Place a small pan over medium heat. Add the whole peppercorns, fennel seeds, and anise seeds. Toast until fragrant.

2. With a mortar and pestle, coarsely crush the peppercorns, fennel, and anise seeds.

3. In a large bowl, combine the pork, crushed spices, salt, sugar, oregano, basil, and wine. Mix thoroughly by hand until it becomes a sticky paste and the spices are uniformly distributed.

4. Cook the sausage fresh and serve or freeze in vacuum-sealed bags for up to 6 months. I like to vacuum seal ½-pound (225-g) portions for uncased ground sausage. If you prefer sausage links, use a sausage stuffer to fill 1- to 1½-inch (2.5- to 3.8-cm) hog casings and tie into 5-inch (12.7-cm) links.

PORK HOCK BARBECUE BEANS

Pork hocks are filled with bone, fat, and connective tissue that lend complex flavors to a pot of beans. Pork hocks are typically sold smoked or cured at a grocery store, but occasionally you can find some fresh.

By butchering at home, I can fabricate meat exactly as I want it. I prefer to freeze my hocks fresh and use them to add depth to dishes like this barbecue bean recipe. If you end up purchasing hocks from a store, don't buy the smoked or cured ones: Only use a fresh hock for this recipe.

Instructions

1. Rinse the beans in a colander and remove any small pebbles, rocks, or debris. Transfer the beans to a large bowl and fill with enough clean water to cover the beans by about 2 inches (5 cm). Cover and allow the beans to soak overnight.

2. Strain the beans.

3. In a large stockpot, combine the beans, onion, jalapeño, red pepper, garlic, fresh ham hock, and 3 quarts (2.8 L) of water. Over medium-high heat, bring everything to a boil, then immediately reduce the heat to medium-low. Cover and simmer for 1 hour, stirring every 15 minutes to make sure the beans are not sticking to the bottom of the pot.

4. Preheat the oven to 350°F (177°C).

5. In a large bowl, combine the molasses, homemade barbecue sauce, brown sugar, Worcestershire sauce, ketchup, Dijon mustard, brown sugar pork rub, and apple cider vinegar.

6. After the bean mixture is done simmering, use a spider strainer to transfer all of the solid contents from the pot to a 10-by-15-inch (25-by-38-cm) casserole dish.

7. Pour 2 cups (420 ml) of the cooking liquid into a fat separator. Allow the liquid to sit for a few minutes until the fats separate from the liquid. Discard the fat, then add the liquid to the casserole dish.

8. Add the sauce mixture to the casserole dish and mix until everything is well combined.

INGREDIENTS

1 pound (455 g) dried navy beans

1 medium sweet onion, finely chopped

1 jalapeño, finely chopped

1 red bell pepper, finely chopped

2 cloves garlic, minced

1 fresh ham hock

3 quarts (2.8 L) water

¼ cup (84 g) molasses

1 cup (250 ml) homemade barbecue sauce (page 95)

¼ cup (59 g) light brown sugar

1 teaspoon Worcestershire sauce

2 tablespoons (22 g) Dijon mustard

¼ cup (153 g) ketchup

¼ cup (150 g) brown sugar pork rub (page 96)

2 tablespoons (30 ml) apple cider vinegar

Chopped scallions for garnish

Prep Time: 20 minutes plus overnight to soak beans
Cook Time: 3 hours
Yield: Serves 8 to 10

9.   Place the dish in the oven and bake for 2 hours. When you
        remove the beans from the oven, they will appear nearly liquid;
        as they cool, they will thicken up.

10.   Discard the pork hocks or, if you prefer some meat in the beans,
        pull the meat away from the skin and bones and stir only the
        shredded meat back into the beans.

11.   Serve garnished with freshly chopped scallions.

BLANCHED BONE PORK STOCK

I like to keep my pork stock simple, with bright flavors like celery and scallions and a hint of black peppercorn. I recommend blanching the bones to remove impurities or funky flavors. If you're butchering any amount of pork at home, you probably have extra scraps and bones that you can freeze until you have enough to make pork stock. Use this stock for things like braising pork and in soups or ramen dishes.

Instructions

1. In a large stockpot, add the pork bones and cover with cold water. Bring to a boil and let them cook at an aggressive simmer for about 20 minutes. Drain and rinse the bones, then discard the water and scum.

2. Place 2 gallons (7.6 L) of water in a clean, large stockpot. Place the blanched pork bones, celery, scallions, peppercorns, and garlic in the pot and bring to a simmer. Add the apple cider vinegar, which helps pull nutrients out of the bones. Do not cover the stockpot and do not let it come to a boil.

3. Keep the stock barely simmering with minimal bubbling for 8 to 12 hours. Add more water as needed to keep the bones and vegetables completely submerged, usually 1 or 2 cups (235 or 475 ml). The flavors will intensify the longer you simmer the bones; for a milder stock, stop at 8 hours.

4. Skim the fat off the top as needed. Never stir the stock.

5. Line a colander with cheesecloth and place it over a large bowl.

6. After 8 to 12 hours of simmering, strain the stock slowly through the prepared colander. Discard any solids and scum at the bottom of the pot.

7. Let the strained broth cool at room temperature for at least an hour before refrigerating overnight.

8. The next day, remove the solidified fat from the surface of the liquid and store the pork stock in the refrigerator for 2 to 3 days, or in the freezer for up to 3 months. I like to store mine in 2 to 4 cup measurements (500 ml to 1 L) in resealable freezer bags for ease of use.

INGREDIENTS

5 pounds (2.3 kg) raw pork bones

2 gallons (7.6 L) water, plus more for blanching

1 cup (52 g) roughly chopped celery

1 cup (52 g) roughly chopped scallions

1 tablespoon (5 g) whole black peppercorns

2 garlic cloves, smashed

1 tablespoon (15 ml) apple cider vinegar

Prep Time: 15 minutes
Cook Time: 8 to 12 hours
Yield: 2 gallons (7.6 L)

RENDERED LEAF LARD

Lard has a high melting point, making it a wonderful choice for flaky pie crusts and pastries. It also has a high smoke point, making it great for sautéing and browning meats.

Leaf lard is found around the pig's kidneys and is considered one of the cleanest fats on the pig, as it produces a mild-tasting lard. I love using lard in desserts, like my pecan pie (page 132).

I didn't grow up around this kind of thing, like rendering fat into lard at home, so I understand that this can feel weird at first. Once I realized that rendering fat at home produces the most beautiful, purest form of "cooking oil," I never looked back. Now I see it as pure gold.

Instructions

1. Dice the lard into small cubes, the smaller the better, as it will render more easily. You can also grind the fat, which can make fast work of achieving the small pieces you're after.

2. Place the fat in a slow cooker set on low.

3. Allow to render, uncovered, for 6 to 8 hours, or as long as needed for the cracklings to audibly crackle and also sink down and rise up again as golden brown nuggets. The longer and slower you render the lard, the milder the flavor will be.

4. Strain the liquid through cheesecloth to remove any solid bits. If you see remaining sediment, strain through the cheesecloth until none remains. In its liquid state, the fat will have a yellowish hue. Once it solidifies, it will be an opaque pure white.

5. Allow the lard to cool until it is solid and white, then transfer to a Mason jar or other container with a tight lid. Store in the refrigerator for up to 1 year.

INGREDIENT

1 pound (455 g) leaf lard

Prep Time: 15 minutes
Cook Time: 8 hours
Yield: 1½ cups (355 ml)

BROWNED BUTTER PECAN PIE WITH LARD CRUST

Fall for me means hunting season. It's also pie season. As the leaves change and the temperatures drop, there's nothing that I love more than returning from a hunt and cozying up next to the wood stove with a slice of pie. Specifically, this pecan pie.

What makes this pie so sinfully good is the flaky lard pie crust and the flavorful filling with browned butter and Kentucky bourbon. I like to top mine with a big dollop of whipped cream.

Instructions

1. In a large bowl, combine the flour, salt, and sugar. Add the cold butter and lard. Use your hands to mix, breaking apart the butter and lard until they become small, gravel-like balls coated in flour.

2. Add the ice water and lightly mix with your hands until the dough just starts to come together.

3. On a lightly floured work surface, use a rolling pin to roll the dough into a long sheet. Using a bench scraper, fold the sheet onto itself. Repeat four or five times, until the dough starts to come together. Be careful not to overwork the dough; if overworked, the butter and lard will melt and cause the dough to be heavy, instead of light and flaky.

4. Wrap the dough in plastic wrap and place it in the fridge to rest for 20 minutes.

5. Lightly grease a 9-by-2-inch (23-by-5-cm) pie plate.

6. On a lightly floured surface, roll the dough so it's about 2 inches (5 cm) bigger than the pie plate on all sides. Gently place the sheet of dough over and into the pie plate.

7. Trim the edges of the dough and then crimp them by pinching with your finger. Put the plate in the freezer to chill for 30 minutes.

INGREDIENTS

For the pie dough:

2¼ cups (282 g) all-purpose flour

1 teaspoon kosher salt

1 tablespoon (13 g) white sugar

½ cup (108 g) very cold unsalted butter, cubed

½ cup (108 g) very cold rendered leaf lard (page 131)

½ cup (118 ml) ice water (start with ⅓ cup [79 ml] and add more as needed), strained

For the filling:

¼ cup (54 g) browned, melted, unsalted butter

½ cup (59 g) pecan halves

¼ cup (80 g) maple syrup

1 cup (326 ml) light corn syrup

¾ teaspoon kosher salt

¾ cup (165 g) light brown sugar

3 eggs

1½ teaspoons bourbon

1½ teaspoons vanilla extract

Whipped cream for serving

Prep Time: 1 hour
Cook Time: 1 hour
Yield: Serves 8

8. In a small pan over medium heat, melt ¼ cup (54 g) of butter, stirring often. As the butter melts and cooks down, it will start to sizzle. When the sizzling starts to calm down, most of the moisture will have been cooked off. The butter will be fragrant and brown in color with brown specks.

9. Reduce the heat to medium-low. Add the maple syrup and corn syrup. Allow it to cook until slightly thickened, about 3 to 5 minutes, stirring frequently.

10. Let the mixture cool for 10 minutes.

11. Preheat the oven to 350°F (177°C).

12. While the mixture is cooling, stir together the brown sugar, salt, eggs, bourbon, and vanilla extract in a medium bowl. Mix until well combined.

13. Slowly whisk in the cooled butter mixture. Set aside.

14. Remove the pie crust from the refrigerator and place the pecans in the bottom of the pan. Pour in the butter-egg mixture. The pecans will float to the top, but make sure they are completely coated.

15. Place inside the oven and bake for 40 to 50 minutes, until the crust is golden and the pecans have browned.

16. Remove the pie from the oven and allow to cool for 2 hours.

17. Serve topped with whipped cream.

Venison

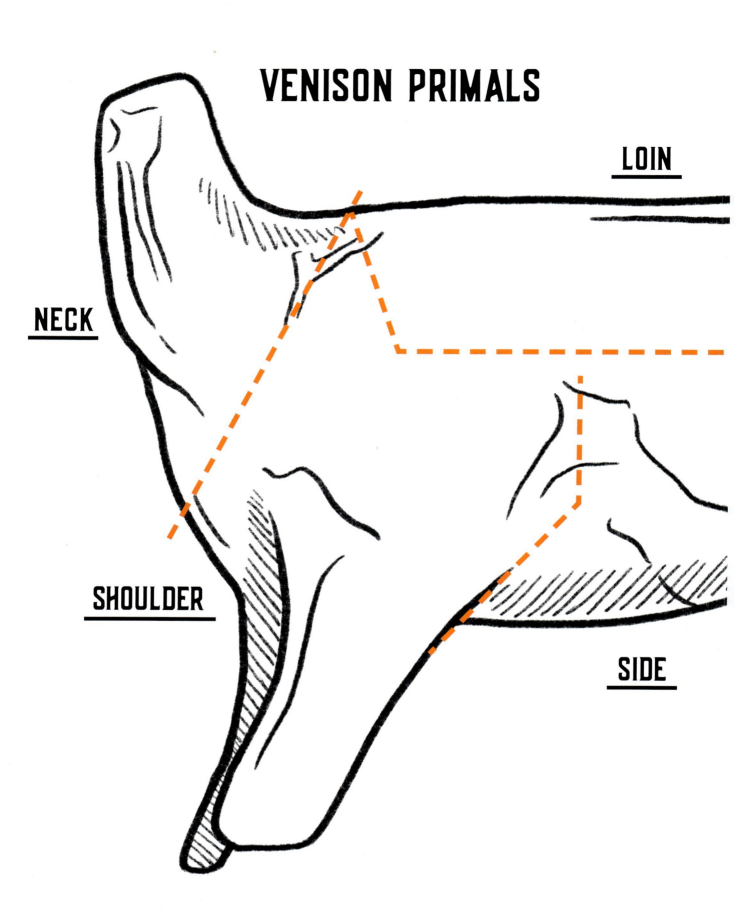

VENISON PRIMALS

LOIN

NECK

SHOULDER

SIDE

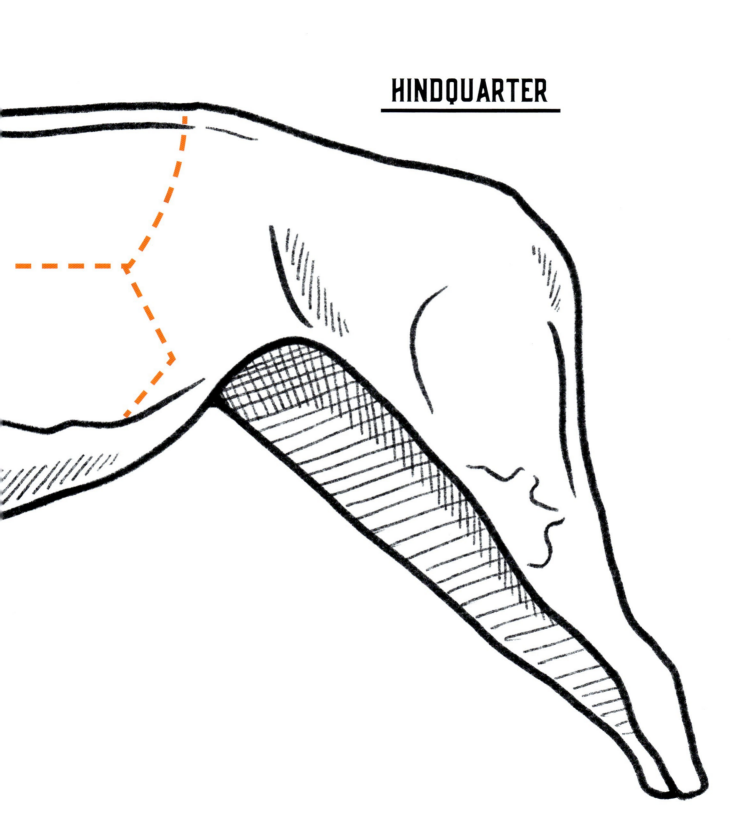

VENISON CUTS EXPLAINED

Venison is lean, rich meat, but it can also be quite tough. Many people find its taste gamy, with a pungent, earthy flavor. When balanced and cooked correctly, though, the meat's gamy flavor becomes highly desirable, enjoyed equally by those with sophisticated palates and by those who simply appreciate good food. Each cut of venison plays by its own rulebook and should be treated accordingly to unlock its fullest potential.

VENISON PRIMALS

The butchering process of a deer begins after the animal has been field dressed and skinned. The standard way to break down a deer is to separate it into large initial cuts of meat, the primals, while it is hanging vertically by the hind legs. Once the primals are separated, the meat can be broken down into smaller cuts that are more manageable, the subprimals. (For more information, see the description of primal and subprimals in the general section on butchery, page 35.)

The list below is not comprehensive, but rather a starting point for you to learn from and gain confidence in your exploration of new cuts of venison.

Keep in mind the age and sex of an animal affects the meat's flavor and tenderness. The meat from a young female doe will be mild in flavor and more tender than the same cut from a mature male buck.

Neck

The neck is a cluster of tough muscles and tendons intertwined in a thick, strong sheath that wraps around the cervical vertebrae of the spine. Because of its toughness, neck meat is best prepared either by long, slow cooking at low temperature or ground into delectable morsels that can be used for sloppy joes (page 182), breakfast sausage (page 177), or lentil soup (page 179). Its ground form is my preferred way to enjoy this cut of meat.

Front Shoulder

Alternate names: arm, chuck, front quarter

The meat from the front shoulder is tough because the muscles are actively used for daily movement. A long, slow cooking method is preferred for tenderizing this tough meat.

There's one exception to this rule: the flat iron. This is a tender cut of meat hidden within the shoulder blade of the deer. Small and triangular, the flat iron is made of two thin muscle groups sandwiching a tough strip of silver skin. It can be a challenge to remove, so be aware of this when deciding to fabricate this cut. On larger game animals, like elk or moose, I find it's worth cutting out, but I leave it on the shoulder of smaller game animals, like whitetail deer.

- **Option 1:** Use the entire front quarter as a bone-in leg roast. This option is great when feeding a large group of people.

- **Option 2:** Remove the flat iron from the shoulder blade and enjoy as tender steaks or keep the shoulder blade as its own bone-in roast. Use the shank for osso buco and braise until fall-apart tender or use as ground meat.

- **Option 3:** Fillet all of the meat from the bones and grind or chop into stew meat.

Loin

Alternate names: backstrap, striploin

The loin of the deer contains some of the most prized and tender cuts of meat from the entire animal. Unlike the loin section of a pig, which can be so mildly flavored some consider it flavorless, the venison loin is rich with flavor and beautifully tender, making it perfect for steaks.

The other cut of meat from the loin section is called the tenderloin. Located on the inside of the cavity, the tenderloins are arguably the best cut of meat from a deer and certainly my personal favorite. All cuts from the loin section are best served medium rare.

Side

Alternate names: flank, belly

The meat found in the side section of the deer is thin, tough, and surrounded by connective tissue and silver skin. It is most often used for ground meat. It includes meat from the ribs, flank, and brisket. I recommend taking the extra time to remove the meat between each rib to increase the yield from the deer.

Hindquarter

Alternate names: round, rump, leg

The hindquarter is the most exciting primal to break down because there are several unique cuts of meat that come from this large, complex group of muscles, more than any other primal on the deer. There are a mix of tender cuts, flavorful roasts, collagen-rich bones, and more, so the possibilities for preparation in the kitchen are endless. All cuts from the hindquarter benefit from marinating or brining.

Subprimals of the Hindquarter

Top Round. The top round is one of the most tender cuts of meat on the hindquarter. Take extra care when processing this cut, as it is more versatile for cooking than other cuts from the hindquarter.

Meat care starts in the field. Avoid splitting the pelvis during the gutting process to prevent contaminating the top round.

You can cut the top round into steaks, slice thin for stir-fry, gently dry for jerky, or cube for stew meat.

Eye of Round. The eye of round is similar in shape to a tenderloin, but it does not have the same tender qualities that the true tenderloin boasts. The eye of round sits somewhere on a spectrum between tender and tough. Brining and roasting the meat goes a long way in showcasing this cut's full potential.

Bottom Round. The bottom round is not a tender cut of meat, so it is best cooked for a long time at low temperature. Its rectangular, even shape makes it easy to slice into strips of jerky, which is my favorite way to prepare this cut. It's also great for stews and pot roasts, and can be used for ground meat.

Sirloin Tip. This rounded, football-shaped cut is my go-to for slow cooking. It's made up of a few different muscle groups that are separated by thin, tough silver skin; these muscles require slow cooking methods to gently break down the tough tissue into rich, fork-tender bites. Because of the silver skin running through the roast, this cut is not a good choice for jerky.

Tri-Tip. This small, tough, triangular muscle sits on top of the sirloin tip. I recommend grinding the meat or leaving it on the sirloin tip as part of a slow-cooked roast.

Sirloin Butt. The sirloin butt wraps around the top side of the pelvis and is a relatively tender cut of meat. It is awkwardly shaped and quite small on a whitetail deer, so I find it best sliced thin against the grain and used for stir-fry. It can also be cubed for stew meat or used for ground meat.

Shank. The shank is made up of multiple tubelike muscles that wrap around the tibia bone of the leg beneath the knee. Because of the connective tissue, tendons, and ligaments that are intertwined with the muscle and bone, the shank is best kept bone-in and slowly braised until the meat is fall-apart tender.

HOW TO BUTCHER A DEER

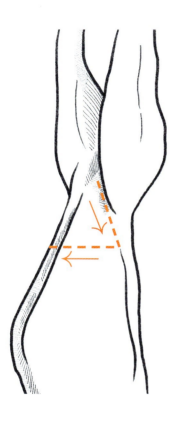

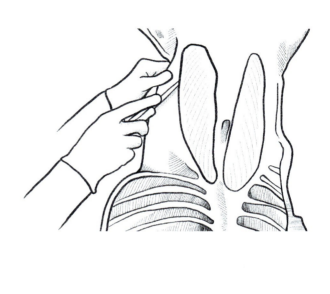

1. **Remove flank meat.** With the deer hanging by both hind legs, start at the groin and cut the flank meat away from the carcass. Make a cut down the side of the deer until you hit the ribs. Trace the rib with your knife until the flank meat is completely removed.

2. **Remove tenderloins.** Locate the insertion point where the tenderloin connects into the hindquarter. Make a horizontal cut at the insertion point. Fillet the meat away from the bone. Take your time here, as the tenderloins are some of the best cuts of meat on the entire animal.

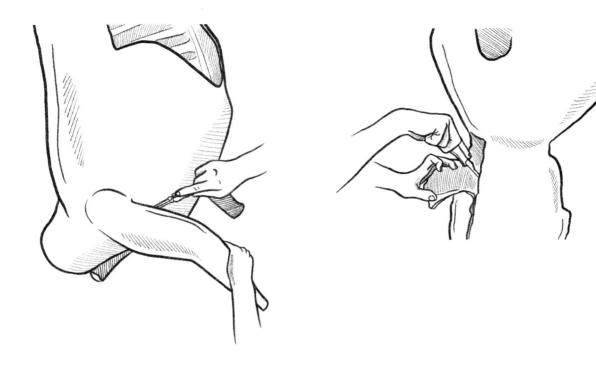

3. **Remove the front legs.** Using your left hand, pull the leg away from the body. Using the tip of your knife, cut through the white connective tissue between the body of the deer and the shoulder until you hit the meat connected to the shoulder blade. Slice through the meat until the shoulder is released from the carcass. Don't worry about cutting through any of the tender meat connecting the shoulder to the body; this is scrap meat and will be ground or used in stews, so you can't ruin any cuts here.

4. **Remove the backstrap (loin).** Starting at the seam where the hindquarter meats the rest of the body, make a horizontal cut on each side of the spine. Make a vertical cut down the spine all the way down to the base of the neck. Using your left hand, pull the backstrap away from the carcass and using the tip of your knife, fillet the backstrap away from the bones of the spine. There are small bones that protrude from the spine that can get in the way of your knife as you cut the backstrap away: Take your time and cut around these to remove as much meat as possible. Make a final horizonal cut at the base of the neck to finish removing the backstrap. Repeat on the other side.

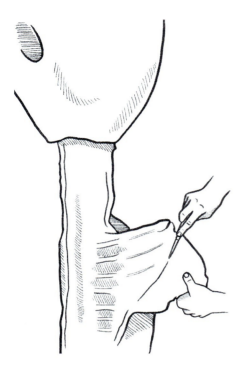

5a.

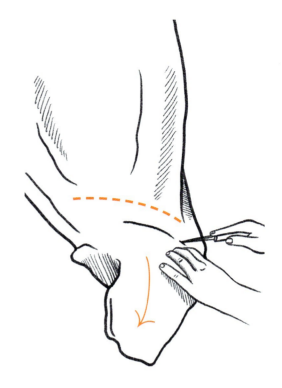

5. **Remove the rib meat.** Using your knife, fillet the meat off the rib cage (see illustration 5a). Cut in between each rib to remove additional meat (see illustration 5b). Repeat on the other side.

6. **Remove the neck meat.** Carve the meat away from the bone on each side of the spine. Repeat on the other side.

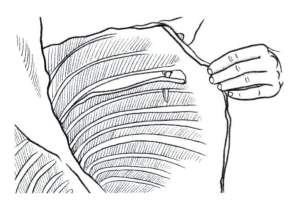

5b.

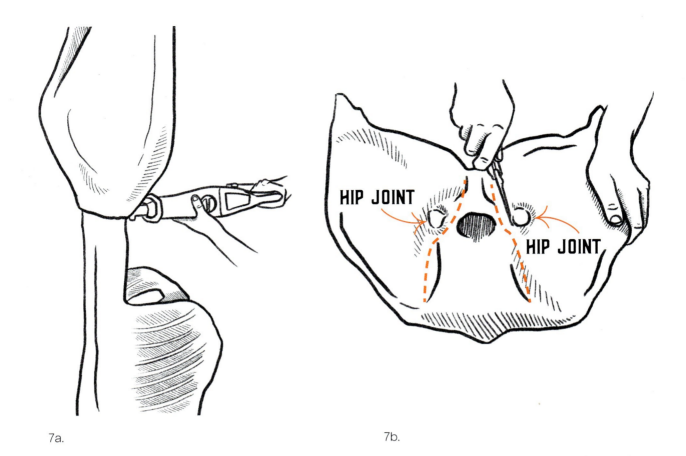

7a.

7b.

7. **Remove the hindquarters.** Using a saw, make a cut where the spine meets the hindquarters at the hip (see illustration 7a). Cut the hindquarter away from the pelvis by filleting the meat away from the bone until you have located the hip joint. Using leverage, pop the hip joint. Use the pelvic bone as a guide to fillet the meat off the bone (see illustration 7b).

Going Further

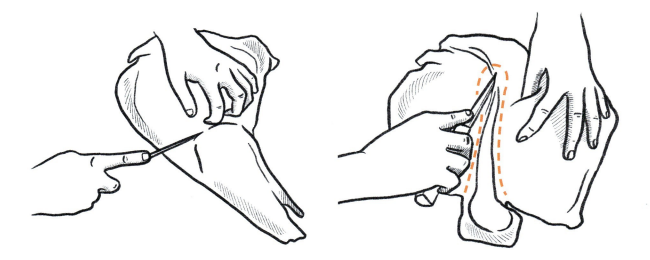

HOW TO BREAK DOWN A HINDQUARTER

1. **Remove the shank.** Cut around the top of the knee where the white connective tissue meets the muscle, just enough to release the muscles of the thigh from the shank. Use your fingers to break the fascia apart. Repeat on the opposite side. Bend the knee joint and cut in the center of the joint where the two bones meat. Using leverage, break the joint. Using your left hand, pull the thigh meat away from the shank meat and fillet the upper shank muscle away from the femur bone.

2. **Remove the femur bone.** Working on the inside of the thigh, cut along the natural seam lines in the center of the hindquarter. Once you reach the femur, fillet the meat away from the bone, using the bone as your guide. Imagine you're scraping the meat off the bone with your knife. Continue cutting until the bone is freed from the meat.

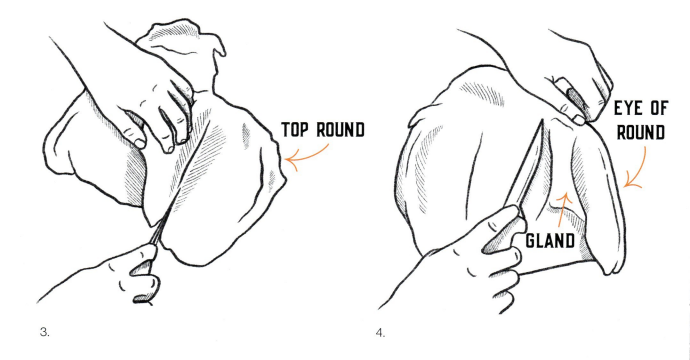

TOP ROUND

EYE OF ROUND

GLAND

3.

4.

3. **Remove the top round (inside round).** Cut away the thin, flat muscle group lying on top of the top round. This meat can be saved for grinding. The top round is now more visible. Cut along the natural seam until the cut of meat is removed completely.

4. **Remove the gland.** Locate the femoral artery and cut it away. The chunk of fat remaining contains a gland that you should be careful to avoid: Cutting directly through this gland can result in off flavors that will spread through the meat. Using your knife, fillet the fat away from the meat and discard.

5. **Remove the eye of round.** This is one of the smaller cuts of meat from the hindquarter. Once located, simply cut along the natural seam to remove it from the other muscle groups.

6. **Remove the bottom round.** The bottom round is a long, rectangular cut of meat connected to the sirloin tip and sirloin butt. Cut along the natural seam lines to remove it.

7. **Remove the sirloin butt.** The sirloin butt is located at the very top of the hindquarter connected to the top of the tri-tip and sirloin tip. Cut along the natural seam to remove it.

8. **Remove the tri-tip.** The tri-tip wraps around the front of the sirloin tip. Cut along the natural seam to remove it.

9. **Remove the sirloin tip.** All that remains is a football-shaped cut of meat called the sirloin tip.

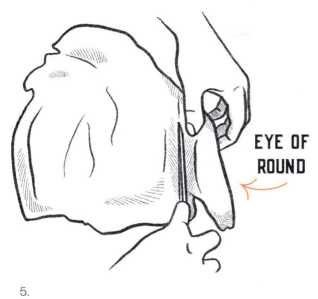

EYE OF
ROUND

5.

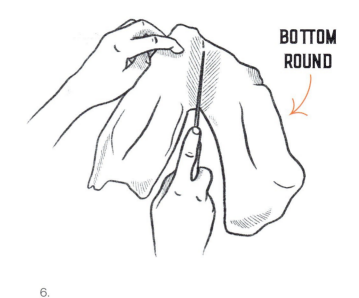

BOTTOM
ROUND

6.

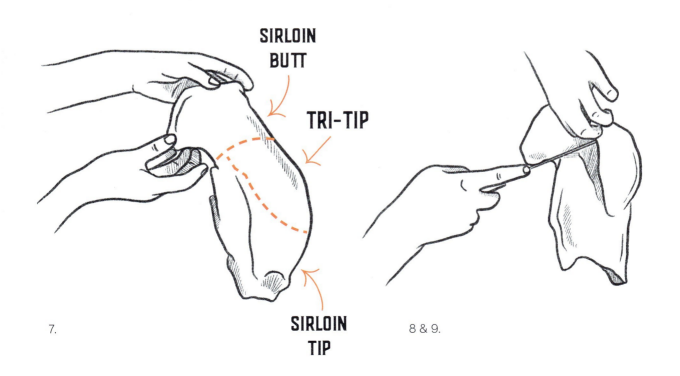

SIRLOIN
BUTT

TRI-TIP

SIRLOIN
TIP

7.

8 & 9.

BONE-IN SHOULDER ROAST

Some of the first cooking techniques I learned when I started hunting deer were brining and slow-roasting meat. A wet brine is great for adding moisture while toning down gamy flavors common with venison. I'd recommend using this recipe on a smaller deer, like a young doe, so that the size is manageable.

Instructions

1. Remove all silver skin and fat from the shoulder roast.

2. In a large stockpot, bring 2 quarts (1.9 L) of water to a boil, along with the sugar, salt, garlic, rosemary, onion, and peppercorns. Let boil for a few minutes until fragrant.

3. Remove the brine from the heat. Add 2 quarts (1.9 L) of cold water. *Important*: Allow the brine to cool down to room temperature.

4. Once the brine has cooled, skim out the herbs and spices and set them aside. Use a meat injector to inject the liquid from the brine into the venison shoulder. Push the needle into the meat at a 45-degree angle, going about 3 inches (7.6 cm) deep. Push the injector to expel the liquid as you pull the needle out. Leave about 2 inches (5 cm) of space between injections. You'll use approximately 3 cups (752 ml) of liquid.

5. Place the shoulder in a deep roasting dish and cover with the brine, ensuring the meat is completely submerged in liquid. Cover and place in the refrigerator for 12 to 24 hours.

6. One hour prior to cooking, remove the venison from the brine, pat very dry with paper towels, and allow it to come to room temperature. This important step helps the meat cook more evenly.

7. Preheat the oven to 350°F (177°C).

8. Pat the venison dry with paper towels. Drizzle with olive oil and season lightly with freshly ground black pepper.

INGREDIENTS

5-pound (2.3 kg) bone-in venison shoulder

For the brine:

4 quarts (3.8 L) water, divided

½ cup (100 g) granulated sugar

1 cup (288 g) kosher salt

1 whole garlic head, halved, skin on

2 rosemary sprigs

1 yellow onion, quartered, skin on

2 tablespoons (10 g) whole peppercorns

2 cups (492 ml) beef or venison stock

1 tablespoon (15 ml) olive oil

For the gravy:

2 tablespoons (28 g) flour

2 cups (492 ml) beef or venison stock

Kosher salt and freshly ground black pepper to taste

Prep Time: 15 minutes plus 12 to 24 hours brining

Cook Time: 5 to 6 hours

Yield: Serves 4 to 6

9. Prepare a roasting pan with a wired rack inside. Place the onion, rosemary, and garlic from the brine at the bottom of the pan. Place venison shoulder on top of the wired rack. Pour in the stock. Cover with aluminum foil.

10. Place the roasting pan in the oven and roast, covered, for 4½ to 5½ hours, until the meat pulls away clean from the bones and is fork tender.

11. Remove the foil and check to see if there is still liquid in the pan. If not, add ¾ cup (175 ml) of water.

12. Raise the oven temperature to 425°F (118°C). Roast for another 20 to 30 minutes, or until the skin is browned and begins to crisp.

13. Transfer the shoulder from the roasting pan to a large cutting board. Pour a few spoonfuls of pan juice over the meat, then set the roasting pan and its contents aside. Cover the meat loosely with aluminum foil and allow it to rest for 30 minutes.

14. To create the gravy, place the roasting pan on the stove over medium-high heat. Use a wooden spoon to stir in the flour. Continue stirring for 30 seconds. Add the stock and stir until well combined.

15. Use a potato masher to lightly mash the onion and garlic, pushing more flavor into the liquid.

16. Simmer the gravy until it begins to thicken, about 3 minutes.

17. Pour gravy through a fine colander to remove any solids, then season kosher salt and freshly ground black pepper to taste.

18. Carve or shred the meat off the bone and serve with gravy.

COFFEE-RUBBED VENISON LOIN CHOPS (BACKSTRAP)

Coffee and red meat may seem an unlikely pair, but this duo combines harmoniously to create one of my all-time favorite wild game dishes. Simple to prepare, with a focus on good technique to create a beautiful crust, this dish hits a high note with richness from the dark roast coffee rub.

You don't have to be a coffee lover to enjoy this recipe. In fact, the coffee doesn't add any coffee flavor. Rather, it helps create a full-bodied base to enhance other flavors in the rub, like chili, smoked paprika, and cumin.

This rub can be doubled or tripled, depending on what you need. I like to make a large batch and keep it in a Mason jar alongside other homemade rubs, like my brown sugar pork rub (page 96).

Instructions

1. Remove all silver skin and fat from the backstrap. Salt the venison liberally with kosher salt. Cover and place in the refrigerator for 12 to 24 hours. Salt applied to the meat in advance makes a big difference in flavor and tenderness. (See page 22 for more information.)

2. Thirty minutes prior to cooking, remove the meat from the refrigerator and allow it to come to room temperature. This important step ensures even cooking.

3. In a small bowl, combine the coffee, brown sugar, chili powder, paprika, cumin, salt, and black pepper. Set aside.

4. Dry all sides of the meat thoroughly with paper towels. This important step helps create a crusty sear. Cover all sides of the meat with seasoning, patting it in with your hands.

5. Heat a large cast-iron pan over medium-high heat for 1 minute. Add the avocado oil and heat for 30 seconds.

INGREDIENTS

4 (4 to 6 ounce; 113 to 170 g) venison loin chops (backstrap steaks)

1 tablespoon (15 g) freshly ground dark roast coffee

1 tablespoon (15 g) light brown sugar

2 teaspoons chili powder

2 teaspoons smoked paprika

1 teaspoon cumin

1 teaspoon kosher salt

1 teaspoon freshly ground black pepper

2 tablespoons (30 ml) avocado oil

1 tablespoon (14 g) unsalted butter

Prep Time: 5 minutes plus 12 to 24 hours tenderizing
Cook Time: 10 minutes
Yield: Serves 4

6. Place the backstrap into the pan. It should sizzle loudly when you first add it. Sear one side for 3 to 4 minutes without touching or moving the meat. Flip and add the butter to the pan. Sear for an additional 3 to 4 minutes, again without touching or moving the meat. Baste the meat with spoonfuls of melted butter.

7. Continue to cook the meat until it reaches an internal temperature of 120°F to 125°F (49°C to 52°C).

8. Remove venison from heat and let rest for 10 minutes.

9.   Slice against the grain and serve.

> **Tip:** Cooking times vary greatly depending on the thickness of your steaks. The suggested 3 to 4 minutes per side is recommended for steaks about 1 inch (2.5 cm) in thickness.

REVERSE-SEARED ROSEMARY LOIN CHOPS (BACKSTRAP) WITH RED WINE REDUCTION

I moved to Idaho after college. I lived in a small town nestled in the Rocky Mountains where the winters were long, cold, and lonely. I was two thousand miles away from my friends and family, so when the sun went down, there wasn't much to do.

That's where my culinary exploration began. After my first successful big game hunt in the West, I had a freezer full of mule deer meat—and no idea how to prepare it. It started with cooking a backstrap on a scratched old Teflon pan on my apartment's electric stove. Even sadly seasoned with table salt and preground black pepper, the venison steak was tasty enough to confirm my love of venison. It also fueled my desire to improve my skills in the kitchen.

This recipe is cathartic. It's a far cry from the venison I cooked in those early days, yet it embodies everything I knew it could be. It's a reflection of my own growth as a person.

Instructions

1. In a large bowl, combine the soy sauce, olive oil, Worcestershire sauce, rosemary, garlic, mustard seeds, and peppercorns.

2. Remove all silver skin and fat from the backstrap. Place the venison in the bowl and completely cover with marinade. Cover the bowl and refrigerate for 2 to 4 hours.

3. Remove the marinade from the refrigerator. Drain and discard the liquid. Place the venison on a plate and allow to come to room temperature on the kitchen counter for at least 30 minutes. This important step ensures even cooking and a juicer end product.

4. Preheat the oven to 275°F (135°C). Place a wire roasting rack onto a rimmed baking sheet.

5. Dry the meat thoroughly with paper towels, then lightly season with kosher salt and freshly ground black pepper.

Continued

INGREDIENTS

For the marinade:

⅓ cup (85 ml) soy sauce

½ cup (109 ml) olive oil

¼ cup (69 g) Worcestershire sauce

1 rosemary sprig

3 fresh garlic cloves

1 tablespoon (9 g) mustard seeds

1 tablespoon (5 g) whole peppercorns

For the venison:

2 venison loin chops (backstrap steaks), about 1½ inches (3.8 cm) thick

Kosher salt and freshly ground black pepper

2 tablespoons (28 g) unsalted butter

2 tablespoons (30 ml) olive oil

Freshly chopped parsley for garnish

Continued

6. Place the venison on the wire rack and place in the oven. Bake until the chops reach an internal temperature of around 105°F (41°C), about 15 to 20 minutes for a 1½-inch (3.8-cm) thick steak. Keep a close eye on the meat after the first 10 minutes and measure its internal temperature with a thermometer until it reaches 105°F (41°C).

7. Once the venison reaches the proper temperature, heat a large cast-iron skillet over medium-high heat. Add 2 tablespoons (30 ml) of olive oil and allow it to heat until it flows like water when the pan is tilted.

8. Dry the cooked venison with paper towels, then sear until a brown crust forms, about 2 minutes per side. The meat should sizzle the moment it hits the pan. Immediately add 2 tablespoons (28 g) of butter and baste as the meat cooks, pouring the melted butter all over the steak as it finishes searing. If needed, work in batches to avoid overcrowding.

9. Transfer the cooked venison to a clean plate and allow to rest at room temperature for 15 minutes.

10. While the venison is resting, place the same cast-iron pan over medium heat, keeping all of the remaining butter and drippings in the pan. Add the garlic, shallots, and rosemary sprig, and cook until softened, 1 to 2 minutes, stirring frequently.

11. Add the red wine and use a wooden spoon to scrape the bottom of the pan, releasing the browned, flavorful bits. Simmer until two thirds of the wine has evaporated, about 5 to 7 minutes.

12. Add the stock and stir until well combined. Simmer over low heat until it reduces to about one third, about 20 to 30 minutes. Stir every few minutes.

13. Add the Dijon mustard and unsalted butter and stir until well combined. Simmer until it reduces to a thickened sauce, another 1 to 2 minutes.

14. Slice the venison against the grain and serve with red wine reduction sauce. Garnish with freshly chopped parsley.

For the red wine reduction sauce:

1 fresh garlic clove, minced

1 small shallot, minced

1 rosemary sprig

1 cup (234 ml) dry red wine

1 cup (246 ml) beef or venison stock

1 tablespoon (11 g) Dijon mustard

2 tablespoons (28 g) unsalted butter

Kosher salt and freshly ground black pepper to taste

Prep Time: 15 minutes plus 2 to 4 hours marinating

Cook time: 1 hour

Yield: Serves 2

WILD MUSHROOM—STUFFED BUTTERFLIED VENISON LOIN (BACKSTRAP)

A butterflied venison loin is a showstopper that I like to save for special occasions and those random weeknights I'm craving an elevated, but easy, dinner. My favorite mushrooms to use for this recipe are wild maitake, foraged by yours truly in the woods of Pennsylvania, but use whatever mushrooms are in season. Morels are another favorite for this recipe; shiitakes or portobellos from the grocery store will also work well.

Instructions

1. Remove all silver skin and fat from the loin. Salt the meat liberally with kosher salt. Cover and place in the refrigerator for 12 to 24 hours. Salt applied to the meat in advance makes a big difference in flavor and tenderness. (See page 22 for more information.)

2. About 30 minutes prior to cooking, remove the venison from the refrigerator and allow it to come to room temperature. This important step ensures even cooking.

3. Heat a medium skillet over medium heat. Melt 2 tablespoons (28 g) of butter, then add the shallot and sauté until the shallot is translucent, about 5 minutes.

4. Add the garlic, fresh thyme, and sage, stirring frequently until they are softened and fragrant, about 1 minute.

5. Stir in the mushrooms and allow to cook until softened, about 5 minutes.

6. Add the sherry. Use a wooden spoon to scrape the bottom of the pan, releasing all of the browned, flavorful bits. Simmer until nearly all of the sherry has evaporated and the mixture has become paste-like, about 5 to 7 minutes.

Continued

INGREDIENTS

1 (2 to 3-pound; 900 g to 1.4-kg) venison loin (backstrap)

Kosher salt

6 tablespoons (85 g) unsalted butter, divided

1 shallot, minced

4 cloves fresh garlic, minced

1 teaspoon fresh thyme, minced

1 teaspoon fresh sage, minced

8 ounces (227 g) chopped wild mushrooms

⅔ cup (156 ml) dry sherry wine

Freshly ground black pepper

Prep Time: 30 minutes plus 12 to 24 hours tenderizing
Cook Time: 2 hours 30 minutes
Yield: 4 to 6 servings

7. Place the venison on a cutting board. With a sharp knife, butterfly the loin by holding your knife parallel to the cutting board, about one third from the bottom of the loin. Slice through the meat, stopping roughly 1 inch (2.5 cm) from the edge. Open the meat like a book and repeat, making another shallow cut until the loin opens completely flat.

8. Dry the meat thoroughly with paper towels, then lightly season all sides with kosher salt and freshly ground black pepper.

9. Preheat the oven to 225°F (107°C). Place a wire roasting rack onto a rimmed baking sheet.

10. Spread the mushroom mixture on one side of the butterflied loin, leaving ½ inch (1 cm) on all sides to avoid the mixture spilling out as it's rolled. Roll the loin and truss it tightly with twine to help it hold its shape and cook evenly. (Find more information on trussing on page 48.)

11. Place the stuffed venison loin onto the wire rack and bake until it reaches an internal temperature of 120°F (49°C), about 1½ hours to 2 hours.

12. Once the venison reaches the proper temperature, heat a large cast-iron skillet over medium heat. After the pan is hot, add the remaining butter and allow it to melt.

13. Pat the outside of the cooked roast dry with paper towels. Place the roast into the skillet and sear until a brown crust forms, about 2 to 3 minutes per side. The moment the meat hits the pan, you should hear sizzling. Use a spoon to baste the meat with the melted butter, constantly pouring it all over the meat as it finishes searing.

14. Transfer the venison roast to a clean cutting board and allow to rest at room temperature for 15 minutes. Slice and serve warm.

GRILLED TENDERLOIN WITH HORSERADISH SAUCE

Beef tenderloin tends to lack flavor, but that's not the case with venison. Venison tenderloin is perfectly balanced with flavor and richness, and it's also smooth because there's no connective tissue running through it.

This recipe is a simple preparation designed to highlight the beauty of this lean, tender cut of meat.

Instructions

1. Remove all silver skin and fat from the tenderloin. Salt the meat liberally with kosher salt. Cover and place in the refrigerator for 12 to 24 hours prior to cooking. Salt applied to the meat in advance makes a big difference in flavor and tenderness. (See page 22 for more information.)

2. About 30 minutes prior to cooking, remove the venison from the refrigerator and allow it to come to room temperature. This important step ensures even cooking.

3. Trim the thin ends, about 1 or 2 inches (2.5 or 3.8 cm) on each side from the tenderloin, in order to shape the meat as evenly in thickness as possible. You can save the thin ends for stir-fry or Mongolian venison (page 165).

4. Place the horseradish in a food processor, along with the rice vinegar. Process until the horseradish looks like finely ground cauliflower. (See Note opposite.) Add the water, 1 or 2 tablespoons (15 or 30 ml) at a time, and continue processing until the horseradish has a smooth, creamy texture. Add small amounts of water as needed.

5. In a medium bowl, combine the horseradish, sour cream, mayonnaise, sugar, chives, and kosher salt. Mix well and then set aside.

6. Preheat a grill on high and allow it to come to temperature.

INGREDIENTS

2 venison tenderloins

Kosher salt and freshly ground black pepper

2-inch (5-cm) horseradish root, peeled and roughly chopped into chunks (about ¾ cup; 189 g)

⅓ cup (82 ml) rice vinegar

¼ cup (59 ml) water

½ cup (116 g) full-fat sour cream

2 tablespoons (28 g) mayonnaise

½ teaspoon granulated sugar

1 tablespoon (3 g) fresh chives, finely chopped

¼ teaspoon kosher salt

Prep Time: 15 minutes plus 12 to 24 hours tenderizing
Cook Time: 10 minutes
Yield: Serves 4

7. Dry the venison thoroughly with paper towels. This will create the best sear for a brown, crusty result. Season thoroughly with kosher salt and freshly ground black pepper.

8. Place the tenderloin on the grill and cook until a golden brown, lightly charred crust forms, about 4 to 5 minutes, depending on the thickness. Don't touch the meat while it is searing.

9. Flip the tenderloin and continue to grill for 3 to 5 minutes. For medium rare, the meat should reach 130°F to 133°F (54°C to 56°C).

10. Remove the meat from the grill and tent with aluminum foil. Allow it to rest for 10 minutes; the temperature will continue to rise during this time to reach 135°F (57°C).

11. Slice the tenderloin and serve with horseradish sauce.

> **Note:** Be cautious during this step: Freshly ground horseradish is potent and can hurt your eyes if you get close or inhale the fumes. The vinegar stabilizes the level of hotness of the fresh horseradish, so the longer you wait to add the vinegar, the hotter it gets. I like to add the vinegar immediately to produce a milder taste, but if you like your horseradish hot, pulse with water and wait a minute or two before adding the vinegar.

ROASTED VENISON STOCK

Venison stock is a no-brainer. When butchering your deer during the hunting season, save all the bones and freeze them until you have time to make stock. I love the femur bones and shoulder blades, but you can use any of the bones from the deer.

This stock is perfect to use in pot roasts, for braising, and for deglazing pan drippings for steak sauce. I like to portion it into 2- to 4-cup bags (600 ml to 1.1 L) and freeze, so it's always ready when I need it.

Instructions

1. Preheat the oven to 450°F (232°C).

2. On a rimmed baking sheet, evenly spread out the venison bones, carrots, celery, onion, and garlic. Use multiple baking sheets as needed to ensure all ingredients are spread in a single layer for even roasting. Don't overcrowd the baking sheet.

3. Place the baking sheet in the oven and roast until the edges of the vegetables are golden brown and the bones have become browned, about 20 to 30 minutes. Toss after 10 minutes to ensure even roasting on all sides.

4. Transfer the roasted bones and vegetables plus all drippings and browned bits from the baking sheet to a large stockpot. Pour in the water, then add the peppercorns and rosemary and bring to a simmer, uncovered.

5. Add the red wine vinegar, which helps pull nutrients out of the bones.

6. Keep the stock barely simmering with minimal bubbling for 8 to 12 hours—do not let it come to a boil. Add more water as needed to keep the bones and vegetables completely submerged, usually 1 to 2 cups (235 to 475 ml). Skim the fat off the top as needed, but never stir the stock.

7. Line a colander with cheesecloth and place over a large bowl.

8. The flavors will intensify the longer you simmer the bones; for a milder-tasting stock, stop at 8 hours.

INGREDIENTS

5 pounds (2.3 kg) raw venison bones

1 cup (85 g) roughly chopped carrots

1 cup (85 g) roughly chopped celery

1 cup (85 g) roughly chopped yellow onion

1 head of garlic, halved

2 gallons (7.6 L) water

1 teaspoon peppercorns

1 fresh rosemary sprig

3 fresh parsley sprigs

1 tablespoon (15 ml) red wine vinegar

Prep Time: 15 minutes
Cook Time: 8 to 12 hours
Yield: 2 gallons (7.6 L)

9. When you feel the stock is ready, strain it through the colander. Discard any solids and scum at the bottom of the pot. Let cool at room temperature for at least 1 hour before refrigerating overnight.

10. The next day, remove the solidified fat from the surface of the liquid. Store the venison stock in the refrigerator for 2 to 3 days, or in the freezer for up to 3 months. For ease of use, I like to freeze mine in 2- to 4-cup measurements (600 ml to 1.1 L) in resealable freezer bags.

HEARTY VENISON POT ROAST

The first time I tried deer I could barely swallow it. The venison stew wasn't properly prepared, but I also couldn't get over the fact that I was eating a deer. I grew up on chicken, pork, and beef, so the idea of eating deer felt so foreign to me, it was hard to chew. It took a few more inexpertly cooked meals before something finally clicked in my head and I became comfortable with the idea of eating wild meat.

This recipe represents the moment I came full circle, to my full appreciation of this meat. It's a nod to the first time I tried venison, just a whole lot better. This dish is as rich in memories from my past as it is in flavors.

Instructions

1. Remove all fat from the sirloin roast. Don't worry about removing silver skin—it will melt away as the roast slowly cooks. Salt your meat liberally with kosher salt. Wrap tightly with plastic wrap and place in the refrigerator for 12 to 24 hours. Salt applied to the meat in advance makes a big difference in flavor and tenderness. (See page 22 for more information.)

2. Thirty minutes prior to cooking, remove the meat from the refrigerator and allow it to come to room temperature. This important step ensures even cooking.

3. Dry the venison thoroughly with paper towels to aid in browning. Season lightly with kosher salt and freshly ground black pepper.

4. Set a large cast-iron pan over medium-high heat. After the pan is hot, add the oil and heat until it flows like water when the pan is tilted.

5. Place the venison into the skillet. The meat should sizzle when you place it in the pan. Brown the venison evenly on all sides, about 2 to 3 minutes per side. Set the browned meat aside.

Continued

INGREDIENTS

1 sirloin roast

Kosher salt and freshly ground black pepper

2 tablespoons (30 ml) olive oil

2 large carrots, chopped

2 celery stalks, chopped

1 medium-size yellow onion, chopped

3 garlic cloves, minced

2½ cups (591 ml) water, divided

4 ounces (132 g) sliced baby portobello mushrooms

¼ cup (47 ml) bourbon

¼ cup (63 ml) soy sauce

1 cup (296 ml) dark roast coffee

1 packet gravy mix

3 tablespoons (48 g) Worcestershire sauce

3 tablespoons (24 g) cornstarch (optional for thickness; see note on page 164)

Prep Time: 15 minutes plus 12 to 24 hours tenderizing

Cook Time: 8 hours

Yield: Serves 6 to 8

6. Reduce the heat to medium. Add the carrots, celery, and onion and sauté until softened, about 10 minutes. Add the garlic and sauté until fragrant, about 1 minute more.

7. Deglaze the pan with ½ cup (118 ml) of water, using a wooden spoon to scrape the brown bits off the bottom of the pan. Pour everything from the pan into a slow cooker.

8. Add the mushrooms, bourbon, soy sauce, coffee, gravy mix, Worcestershire sauce, and remaining water. Stir until everything is well combined.

9. Place the venison on top of the vegetables and cook on low until the meat easily shreds, about 7 to 8 hours.

10. Remove the cooked roast from the slow cooker and place onto a clean cutting board. Cut the roast in half and use two forks to shred the meat.

11. Serve over buttery mashed potatoes with freshly chopped parsley.

Note: This pot roast is meant to have a liquid broth, but if you want it to be thicker, add 3 tablespoons (24 g) of cornstarch to 2 tablespoons (30 ml) of water in a small bowl. Mix until well combined. Add the cornstarch water mixture to the slow cooker and stir. The liquid will begin to thicken after just a few minutes.

MONGOLIAN VENISON

The top (also known as inside) round of an animal comes from the *inside* of the hindquarter. It's a tasty but very lean cut, which means it benefits from some time in a marinade.

I like to use a combination of oil and soy for this recipe, as it goes with the "Mongolian-style" sauce. If this is new to you, it's a bold, salty-and-sweet, soy-based stir-fry. It's not spicy, but I think the powerful flavors of ginger and garlic make it downright addictive.

Instructions

1. Remove all silver skin and fat from the top round. Slice the venison into ¼-inch (6-mm) strips against the grain. (The grain consists of long fibers that run the length of the meat; cut perpendicular to these lines.) This type of cut will create a better texture in the finished dish.

> **Tips for prepping and slicing:** If you have time, salt your venison (before slicing) with kosher salt, wrap tightly with plastic wrap, and place in the refrigerator for 12 to 24 hours prior to cooking. Salt applied to the meat in advance makes a big difference in flavor and tenderness.
>
> After it's prepared, try freezing the meat for a short time before slicing. The meat will firm up, making it easier to cut thin.

2. Combine the sliced meat with 1 tablespoon (15 ml) each of avocado oil and soy sauce in a large, resealable plastic bag. Seal the bag, then shake and massage the mixture through the bag until each piece of meat is completely coated. Flavors infuse faster at room temperature, so leave the bag on the counter to marinate for 30 minutes before cooking. You will also want the meat to reach room temperature before you put it in a hot pan: This will allow for even cooking and a juicer end product.

Continued

INGREDIENTS

For the marinade:

1 top (inside) round venison steak, weighing approximately 1 pound (455 kg)

1 tablespoon (15 ml) avocado oil

1 tablespoon (15 ml) low-sodium soy sauce

¼ cup (96 g) cornstarch, for dredging

For the sauce:

½ cup (110 g) dark brown sugar

⅓ cup (79 ml) water

⅓ cup (88 ml) low-sodium soy sauce

1 teaspoon red pepper flakes

2 tablespoons (30 ml) avocado oil

2 teaspoons minced fresh ginger

1 clove garlic, minced

1 tablespoon (8 g) cornstarch, optional, for thickening

For serving:

Chives, for garnish

White rice, for serving

Prep Time: 30 minutes
Cook Time: 15 minutes
Yield: Serves 4

3. While the meat marinates, combine the brown sugar, water, soy sauce, and red pepper flakes in a small bowl. Set aside.

4. After 30 minutes, discard the marinade liquid and pat the meat dry. Dredge it in the cornstarch until lightly coated. The cornstarch will transform from white to pinkish in color.

5. Heat a large cast-iron pan over medium-high heat for 2 minutes. Once the pan is hot, add 2 tablespoons (30 ml) of avocado oil and allow oil to heat for 30 seconds.

6. Add the venison to the pan in a single, even layer. Cook for 30 seconds, flip, and cook for another 30 seconds. A pair of barbecue tongs works well for this. Remove the meat and place on a sheet pan or extra dinner plate. If the pan begins to look dry, add extra oil as needed and continue to fry the next batch of meat.

   Note: Do not overcrowd the pan, as you want a crisp, caramelized crust on each piece. Crowding the pan will keep the meat from searing properly.

7. Once all the meat has been cooked and you have removed it from the pan, reduce the heat to medium but leave the residual cooking oil in the pan. Add the ginger. After about 30 seconds, add the garlic. Once the aroma of ginger and garlic hits your nose, add the premixed sauce. Stir occasionally while you let it get hot. You'll know you have it right when the sauce softly bubbles as it simmers. This process takes time; be patient with it.

8. If the sauce isn't thickening, create a cornstarch slurry by mixing 1 teaspoon of cornstarch with 1 teaspoon of cold water. Stir until all of the cornstarch is dissolved. The cornstarch will create clumps in your sauce if you don't create the slurry before adding it to the pan. Continue to simmer the sauce until it reaches the desired thickness.

9. Add the venison back to the pan and toss everything together until the meat is well coated.

10. Plate and garnish with chopped chives. Serve immediately with white rice.

ROASTED EYE OF ROUND WITH PEPPERCORN SAUCE

Buttermilk is a fermented dairy liquid, with a thick, somewhat acidic taste and texture. Because of this, marinating meat in buttermilk is a great way to tenderize it and add flavor.

The eye of round is a beautiful, lean cut of meat that closely resembles a tenderloin. But don't be fooled: It's not nearly as tender. Because the eye of round does not contain any connective tissue throughout, it's a great piece of meat to roast and slice. For grilling, though, it needs a strong marinade to work out the toughness and tenderize the cut. The buttermilk's low pH breaks down the tough meat to tenderize and flavor it from within.

Preparing the eye of round requires low, gentle cooking and a strong marinade to transform the meat into something pleasant to sink your teeth into.

Instructions

1. Remove all silver skin from the eye of round roasts.

2. In a large bowl, combine the buttermilk, kosher salt, and brown sugar. Mix until well combined. Stir in the garlic, cloves, sage, and peppercorns.

3. Add the eye of round roasts to the bowl, making sure all sides of the meat are well coated. Cover and put in the refrigerator for 12 to 24 hours.

4. Remove the meat from the marinade and rinse. The meat will look a little discolored when it comes out of the marinade, but that's normal. Dry the meat thoroughly with paper towels. Discard marinade.

5. Allow the meat to come to room temperature on the counter.

6. Preheat the oven to 250°F (121°C). Place a wire roasting rack on a rimmed baking sheet.

Continued

INGREDIENTS

2 eye of round roasts

2 tablespoons (30 ml) olive oil

For the marinade:

2 cups (484 ml) buttermilk

3 tablespoons (69 g) kosher salt

1 tablespoon (15 g) brown sugar

2 garlic cloves, peeled and smashed

2 whole cloves

1 fresh sage leaf

1 tablespoon (5 g) whole peppercorns

For the peppercorn sauce:

1 tablespoon (14 g) unsalted butter

1 shallot, grated

1 clove garlic, minced

1½ tablespoons (7.2 g) whole black peppercorns, coarsely crushed in a mortar

½ cup (123 ml) beef or venison stock

1 teaspoon Worcestershire sauce

1 cup (235 ml) heavy cream

Prep Time: 5 minutes plus 12 to 24 hours marinating

Cook Time: 1 hour 30 minutes

Yield: Serves 4 to 6

7.   Place the meat on the wire rack and place in the oven until the internal temperature reaches 120°F (49°C), 30 minutes to 1 hour, depending on the thickness of the meat

8.   Once the meat reaches the appropriate temperature, remove it from the oven.

9.   Heat a large cast-iron skillet over medium-high heat. After the pan is hot, add the oil and heat until it flows like water when the pan is tilted.

10.   Add the roasts to the pan and sear on all sides, achieving a brown crust of flavor.

11.   Remove the meat from the pan, but keep the drippings in the skillet. Reduce the heat to medium and add the butter.

12.   Sauté the shallots in the melted butter until they're translucent, 3 to 4 minutes. Add the garlic and crushed peppercorns and sauté for 30 seconds, stirring to make sure the garlic does not burn.

13.   Pour in the stock and scrape the bottom of the pan.

14.   Add Worcestershire sauce and then the cream and reduce to a simmer. Let the sauce thicken, about 10 to 12 minutes.

15.   Slice the venison thinly against the grain and serve with peppercorn sauce.

SIRLOIN BUTT STIR-FRY

The sirloin butt is a cut found on the top of the hindquarter of a deer. Tender but awkwardly shaped and too small for steaks, it's the perfect cut for stir-fry. This underrated cut of venison is never better than when it's sliced thin and drenched in a sweet-and-savory sauce. The baby bok choy, red pepper, and snow peas add a freshness that balances out the savory slices of venison.

Instructions

1. Remove all silver skin and fat from the sirloin butt. Salt the meat liberally with kosher salt. Cover and place in the refrigerator for 12 to 24 hours. Salt applied to the meat in advance makes a big difference in flavor and tenderness. (See page 22 for more information.)

2. Twenty minutes before you're ready to cook, throw the meat in the freezer. This will allow the meat to firm up, making it easy to cut into thin slices.

3. Slice the venison into ¼-inch (6 mm) strips against the grain. (The grain consists of long fibers that run the length of the meat; cut perpendicular to these lines.)

4. After slicing, allow the meat to sit on the counter and come to room temperature. This important step ensures even cooking.

5. In a large bowl, combine the oyster sauce, rice vinegar, sesame oil, soy sauce, and brown sugar. Set aside.

6. Place the cornstarch onto a plate large enough for dredging.

7. Pat the meat dry with paper towels, then coat it on all sides with the cornstarch dredge.

8. Heat a large cast-iron pan over medium heat. Once the pan is hot, add the avocado oil and allow it to heat for 30 seconds.

Continued

INGREDIENTS

1 pound (455 g) venison sirloin butt, cut into thin slices

Kosher salt and freshly ground black pepper

¼ cup (32 g) cornstarch, for dredging

2 tablespoons (30 ml) avocado oil

For the sauce:

3 tablespoons (45 g) oyster sauce

1½ tablespoons (21 ml) rice vinegar

1½ teaspoons sesame oil

3 tablespoons (42 ml) low-sodium soy sauce

3 tablespoons (45 g) dark brown sugar

¼ cup (59 ml) water

Juice from 1 lime

Continued

9. Add the venison to the pan in a single, even layer. Cook for 30 seconds, flip, and cook for another 30 seconds. A pair of barbecue tongs works well for this. If the pan begins to look dry, add extra oil as needed and continue to fry the next batch of meat. Do not overcrowd the pan, as you want a crisp, caramelized crust on each piece; crowding the pan will inhibit the meat from searing properly. Remove the meat from the pan and set aside.

10. Reduce the heat to medium, but leave the residual cooking oil in the pan. Add the garlic and ginger and cook for about 30 seconds. Add the jalapeño and red pepper. Cook for 1 minute, then add the snow peas and bok choy. Cook for an additional 2 to 3 minutes until everything is softened. Set aside.

11. With the heat still on medium, deglaze the pan with ¼ cup (60 ml) of water. Use a wooden spoon to scrape all of the browned bits of flavor off the bottom of the pan. Add the sauce mixture and stir. Bring the mixture to a boil, then immediately reduce to a simmer. Allow the sauce to reduce by about half, which should take to 20 minutes. You'll know you have it right when the sauce softly bubbles as it simmers. This process takes time; be patient with it.

12. Add the venison and vegetables back to the pan and toss everything together until it's well coated. Pour in the fresh lime juice and cook over low heat for 1 additional minute.

13. Plate and garnish with chopped scallions and toasted sesame seeds. Serve immediately.

For the stir-fry:

4 cloves fresh garlic, minced

1 tablespoon (6 g) minced fresh ginger

1 large jalapeño, minced

1 large red pepper, julienned

1 cup (85 g) snow peas, stems removed and cut in half lengthwise

1 bunch baby bok choy, sliced into ½-inch (1.3-cm) strips

Fresh scallions chopped for garnish

Toasted sesame seeds for garnish

Prep Time: 30 minutes plus 12 to 24 hours for tenderizing
Cook Time: 30 minutes
Yield: Serves 2

BRAISED VENISON SHANKS

The old expression, "high on the hog," is how butchers described the tenderness of a cut of meat. The most desirable cuts of meat come from higher up on the animal, in the loin section, and the lower you go on the animal, the tougher the meat gets. The shank, sometimes referred to as osso buco, is no exception to that rule.

Shanks are located as low as you can go on a deer and are tough, with a lot of connective tissue and tendons. But don't let that scare you off: Shanks are also one of the most flavorful cuts of meat on the animal. The key to unlocking their potential is in the way you cook them. And this recipe is my all-time favorite way to transform venison shanks into luxurious, fall-off-the-bone-tender meat.

Instructions

1. Salt the venison liberally with kosher salt. Cover and place in the refrigerator for 12 to 24 hours. Salt applied to the meat in advance makes a big difference in flavor and tenderness. (See page 22, for more information.)

2. About 30 minutes prior to cooking, remove the venison from the refrigerator and allow it to come to room temperature. This important step ensures even cooking.

3. Dry the venison thoroughly with paper towels to aid in browning. Season lightly with kosher salt and freshly ground black pepper.

4. Preheat the oven to 350°F (177°C).

5. Set a Dutch oven over medium-high heat. Add the olive oil and heat until it flows like water when the pan is tilted.

6. Add the venison to the pan. It should sizzle immediately. Brown the venison evenly on all sides, about 2 to 3 minutes per side. Work in batches, if needed, to avoid overcrowding; this will help create the desired crust. Once the meat is brown, set it aside.

7. Reduce the heat to medium and add the carrots, celery, and onion and sauté until softened, about 10 minutes. Add the garlic and herbs and sauté until fragrant, about 1 minute.

Continued

INGREDIENTS

4 bone-in venison shanks

Kosher salt and freshly ground black pepper to taste

½ cup (109 ml) olive oil

1 cup (85 g) finely chopped carrots

1 cup (85 g) finely chopped celery

1 cup (85 g) finely chopped onion

⅔ cup (158 g) minced garlic cloves (about 15 whole cloves)

5 sprigs fresh thyme

1 bay leaf

2 cups (468 ml) dry red wine

4 cups (984 ml) beef stock

For the gremolata:

½ cup (118 g) chopped fresh parsley

1 tablespoon (10 g) grated fresh garlic

2 tablespoons (12 g) grated fresh lemon peel

Prep Time: 15 minutes plus 12 to 24 hours tenderizing

Cook Time: 3½ hours

Yield: Serves 2 to 4

8. Pour in the wine and use a wooden spoon to scrape the brown bits off the bottom of the pan. Set the venison on top of the vegetables and herbs. Add the stock, increase the heat to high, and bring to a boil. The liquid should go one-third of the way up the meat.

9. Cover and place in the oven. Cook until the shanks are tender and fall apart at the touch of a fork, about 3 hours. If they aren't tender, continue cooking and check the tenderness every 15 minutes.

10. Meanwhile, in a small bowl, mix together the parsley, garlic, and lemon until well combined. Cover and place in the refrigerator until you're ready to serve.

11. Remove the meat from the oven and skim away any fat from the pan. Discard the thyme and bay leaf.

12. Serve the shanks with mashed potatoes, vegetables, and the braising liquid. Top with fresh gremolata.

MAPLE VENISON BREAKFAST SAUSAGE PATTIES

This dish is fragrant, sweet, and irresistible on a plate next to farm-fresh eggs and homemade hashbrowns. What makes this recipe special is the use of fresh herbs and real maple syrup. The syrup gives the venison patties the American breakfast sweetness that we know and love (don't try to save money: Use *real* maple syrup).

When choosing venison meat to grind, go for meat from the front shoulder or neck. And when choosing pork, go for fatty cuts of meat from the front shoulder or belly. Adding pork is an absolute necessity to create a juicy, fatty sausage-like experience (without it, you'll have sad, dry venison patties).

Instructions

1. In a small bowl, mix the kosher salt, black pepper, sage, thyme, rosemary, fennel, red pepper flakes, and nutmeg until well combined.

2. Cut the venison and pork into chunks that will fit into your meat grinder, then evenly spread out the meat on a baking sheet. Sprinkle the spice mixture evenly across the meat.

3. Place the baking sheet in the freezer for 20 to 30 minutes. Also place the grinder parts in the freezer until just before you're ready to use: It's a lot easier to grind meat when everything is cold.

4. Remove the grinder parts from the freezer and assemble according to the manufacturer's instructions, then remove the meat from the freezer.

5. Grind the meat using a coarse grind. Run the meat through the grinder again using a finer grind. Refreeze the meat as needed to avoid difficulty grinding.

6. In a large bowl, use your hands to mix the ground seasoned meat with brown sugar and maple syrup until well combined. Shape the meat into patties of your preferred size. I recommend making them thinner and larger than you think is right, because they will shrink by about 20 percent when cooked.

Continued

INGREDIENTS

1 tablespoon (23.2 g) kosher salt

1 teaspoon freshly ground black pepper

1 tablespoon (2.2 g) finely chopped fresh sage

2 teaspoons finely chopped fresh thyme

1 teaspoon finely chopped fresh rosemary

½ teaspoon ground fennel powder

½ teaspoon red pepper flakes

⅛ teaspoon nutmeg

1½ pounds (700 g) venison

1 pound (455 g) pork

1 tablespoon (15 g) light brown sugar

1 tablespoon (20 g) real maple syrup

1 tablespoon (14 g) unsalted butter

Prep Time: 45 minutes
Cook Time: 15 minutes
Yield: Serves 8 to 10

7.   Set a large pan over medium heat. After the pan is hot, add the butter and allow it to heat until it flows like water when the pan is tilted.

8.   Place the venison patties in the pan and sauté until brown and cooked thoroughly, 3 to 5 minutes per side. The venison should sizzle when you place it in the pan and continue sizzling until you remove it. Serve immediately.

     Note: Instead of making the ground meat into sausage patties, you can also cook it and use it in other dishes (like in a breakfast burrito).

MR. DELP'S LENTIL SOUP

Before Nick and I moved to Florida, we used to spend our winters there at my father-in-law's place. One of our family friends, Mr. Delp, would come to the house to hang out, talk baseball, and sip bourbon. Mr. Delp and I would often talk about our love of cooking. One time he offered to teach me his lentil soup recipe, which was passed down from his Italian mother. I couldn't resist the offer, so we spent the next day cooking, then enjoying, his lentil soup. Traditionally it's made with Italian sausage, but that night we made it with wild game meat.

This is Mr. Delp's recipe, spiced up with my own spin on it.

Instructions

1. Rinse the lentils with cold water, then place them in a large pot and cover with cold water. Soak the lentils for 12 to 24 hours.

2. Thirty minutes prior to cooking, remove the meat from the refrigerator and allow it to come to room temperature. This important step ensures even cooking.

3. Dry the venison thoroughly with paper towels to aid in browning. Season with onion powder, garlic powder, and kosher salt.

4. Drain the lentils and rinse with cold water. Set aside.

5. Set a Dutch oven over medium heat. After the pan is hot, add ¼ cup (60 ml) olive oil and allow to heat until it flows like water when the pan is tilted. Add the venison to the same pan and brown evenly on all sides, about 5 minutes total. The venison should sizzle when you place it in the pan. Don't overcrowd the pan. If needed, brown the meat in batches. Once the meat is brown, set it aside.

6. Add the remaining 2 tablespoons (30 ml) of olive oil to the pan and allow it to heat up. Add the onions and sauté until softened and translucent, about 10 minutes.

Continued

INGREDIENTS

1 pound (455 g) dry brown lentils

1 pound (455 g) ground venison

½ teaspoon onion powder

½ teaspoon garlic powder

½ teaspoon kosher salt

¼ cup (60 ml) plus 2 tablespoons (30 ml) olive oil, divided

1 yellow onion, finely chopped

3 cloves fresh garlic

1 cup (236 ml) red wine

4 cups (946 ml) homemade chicken stock (page 75)

1 bay leaf

1 (28-ounce; 800-g) can diced tomatoes

1 cup (79 g) shredded Pecorino Romano cheese; I prefer Locatelli

Fresh parsley for garnish

Prep Time: 45 minutes plus 12 to 24 hours soaking lentils
Cook Time: 15 minutes
Yield: Serves 8 to 10

7.   Add the garlic and allow it to sweat (the moisture will be drawn out, softening the cloves) for about 1 minute.

8.   Pour in the wine. Use a wooden spoon to scrape the brown bits off the bottom of the pan.

9.   Add the chicken stock, lentils, and bay leaf. Increase the heat to high and bring to a boil. Cover and immediately reduce the heat to a low simmer. Stir the lentils frequently to keep them from sticking to the bottom of the pan. Allow them to simmer until nearly tender, about 40 minutes.

10. Add the venison and diced tomatoes with the liquids from the can (see note). Allow to simmer for a few minutes, until the venison is warmed.

11. Turn the heat off and add the shredded cheese. Stir and allow the radiant heat to melt the cheese.

12. Serve warm garnished with freshly chopped parsley.

> **Note:** Hold off adding the tomatoes until the lentils are tender. The acid from the tomatoes can toughen the lentils if added too soon.

SLOPPY JOES

In the hunting community, it's so common to prepare sloppy joes from ground venison that hunters have dubbed them "sloppy does." It's a recipe I've tweaked over the years, and these are officially the best sloppy joes I've ever had.

It's sweet but has a surprising depth thanks to the rub mixture and rich caramelized onions. If you are serving venison to a friend for the first time, this recipe is a surefire way to have them asking for more.

Instructions

1. Remove the venison from the refrigerator and set it on the counter top for about 30 minutes to allow it to come to room temperature. This important step ensures even cooking.

2. In a small bowl, combine the black pepper, kosher salt, paprika, coriander, dill weed, red pepper flakes, and dried mustard. Set aside.

3. Heat a large, deep skillet over medium-low heat. Add 1 tablespoon (15 ml) of olive oil and allow to heat. Add the onions and cook until they are just barely browned all the way through, about 45 minutes, stirring every few minutes. You want to move the onions around enough so they don't burn, but let them stay in one place long enough to turn brown. We will continue cooking the onions down with other ingredients.

   Note: Caramelizing onions is a slow process that takes time but is well worth the flavor created.

4. While the onions are caramelizing, place the ground meat in a large bowl and pat dry with paper towels. Add half of the seasoning mix to the meat and mix until well combined. I find it easiest to combine with your hands (make sure to wash them thoroughly after).

Continued

INGREDIENTS

1 pound (455 g) ground venison

1 teaspoon freshly ground black pepper

1 teaspoon kosher salt

1 teaspoon paprika

½ teaspoon ground coriander

½ teaspoon dried dill weed

½ teaspoon crushed red pepper flakes

½ teaspoon dried mustard

3 tablespoons (44 ml) olive oil, divided

1 medium sweet onion, finely chopped

5 cloves garlic, minced

1 red bell pepper, finely chopped

1 cup (244 ml) tomato sauce

2 tablespoons (32 g) tomato paste

2 tablespoons (30 g) light brown sugar

1 teaspoon Worcestershire sauce

1 cup (237 ml) water

1 tablespoon (15 ml) apple cider vinegar

1 tablespoon (14 g) of butter per roll, for toasting

Rolls for serving

Prep Time: 10 minutes
Cook Time: 1 hour 20 minutes
Yield: Serves 2 to 4

5. Heat a medium cast-iron skillet over medium-high heat. Once the pan is hot, add the remaining 2 tablespoons (30 ml) of olive oil. Once the olive oil begins to smoke slightly, add the ground meat in a thin layer—be sure not to overcrowd the pan. The meat should sizzle the moment it hits the pan and continue sizzling until the meat is completely browned with a golden crust. If the meat stops sizzling, it's boiling instead of sautéing, which we don't want. Brown the meat in batches, then set aside.

6. Once the onions are caramelized, add the minced garlic to the pan and cook until fragrant, about 30 seconds. Add the red bell pepper and allow to cook down until they begin to get soft, about 5 minutes.

7. Add the tomato sauce, tomato paste, light brown sugar, Worcestershire sauce, and water. Stir in the meat and the remaining seasoning mix. Stir to combine and simmer for 15 minutes.

8. Add the apple cider vinegar for the last 1 or 2 minutes of cooking.

9. In a large skillet over medium heat, melt the butter. Place the rolls on the pan cut-side down and toast for about 30 seconds until the buns are golden brown. Season with a pinch of kosher salt.

10. Place the desired amount of meat onto a roll and serve.

ROOT BEER VENISON JERKY

Venison jerky is incredibly popular among hunters because it's easy to share. After all, one of the best parts about being a hunter is the ability to share the meat you harvest with friends and family.

The only problem is, most venison jerky doesn't actually taste that good. It's a far cry from the flavorful beef jerky we're used to buying at the supermarket.

This recipe, on the other hand, is a genuinely delicious way to make venison jerky. You'll be proud to share this one. Since venison is a naturally lean meat, it lends itself well to this cooking method. In fact, fattier cuts don't work because fat becomes rancid over time.

My jerky recipe is sweetened by root beer and dark brown sugar and rounded out with heat from cayenne.

Instructions

1. Remove all silver skin, connective tissue, and fat from the roast. The fat will go bad, even after the dehydration process, so it's important to remove all of it. The silver skin and connective tissue are tough and unpleasant to eat.

2. Identify the grain of the meat, its muscle fibers. The fibers on the bottom round are long, running the entire length of the meat. Imagine you're cutting steaks from the bottom round and slice the meat into 1½-inch (3.8-cm) strips against the grain (cutting perpendicular to it).

3. Lay the strips flat and slice again, this time into ⅛- to ¼-inch (3 to 6 mm) thick strips. Consistency is the key here: Each piece of jerky should be the same thickness so that everything cooks evenly.

4. In a 1-quart (900 ml) saucepan, combine the root beer, dark brown sugar, Worcestershire sauce, kosher salt, black pepper, onion powder, garlic powder, and cayenne. Bring to a boil, then immediately reduce to a simmer for 25 minutes. It will reduce by half, to about 1 cup (237 ml) of liquid. Allow to cool completely.

Continued

INGREDIENTS

1 bottom round roast

2 cups (478 ml) root beer

1 tablespoon (15 g) dark brown sugar

1 tablespoon (16 g) Worcestershire sauce

2 tablespoons (44.7 g) kosher salt

1 tablespoon (6 g) freshly ground black pepper

1 teaspoon onion powder

1 teaspoon garlic powder

½ teaspoon cayenne pepper powder

Prep Time: 25 minutes plus overnight for marinating
Cook Time: 4 to 4½ hours
Yield: Serves 2 to 4

5. Transfer the cooled marinade to a large bowl. Add the meat and mix everything with your hands, making sure each venison strip is well coated on all sides.

6. Cover with plastic wrap and refrigerate to marinate overnight. The next day, remove the meat from the marinade and discard the remaining liquid.

7. Preheat smoker to 165°F (74°C).

   Note: You can also do this in an oven set on the lowest temperature or in a dehydrator set to 165°F (74°C). If using an oven, try to keep the door cracked so the moisture can escape; place a fan pointing into the crack to encourage airflow.

8. Rinse the strips with cold water, then thoroughly dry with paper towels. The cooking process will take a lot longer if you don't remove the excess moisture on the outside of the meat and the texture of the jerky will be off if the marinade is not rinsed.

9. Lay out the meat strips in a single, even layer on a wire rack. Smoke for 2 hours, then flip.

10. Increase the smoker temperature to 185°F (85°C) and continue cooking for another 2 to 2½ hours, or until the meat's internal temperature reaches 158°F to 160°F (70°C to 71°C). The jerky will reduce in size and the color will darken to a deep mahogany. You'll start to notice some splitting along the edges. The thicker your jerky, the longer it will take to cook. Watch closely: Over-cooked jerky can become as dry as cardboard.

11. Remove the jerky from the smoker and let cool. The jerky will keep in the refrigerator for 1 week, or you can portion and freeze the jerky for up to 6 months. Store in Mason jars, plastic bags, or vacuum seal in the fridge. If you are going to freeze the jerky, opt for freezer-safe plastic bags or vacuum seal.

RESOURCES

Cutting Boards
John Boos – www.johnboos.com

Cookware
All-Clad – www.all-clad.com
Le Creuset – www.lecreuset.com

Cast iron
Lodge Cast Iron – www.lodgecastiron.com

Kitchen knives
Wüsthof – www.wusthof.com
Lamson – www.lamsonproducts.com

Butchering and field processing knives
Cold Steel – www.coldsteel.com

Meat processing equipment
LEM – www.Lemproducts.com
Weston – www.westonbrands.com

Vacuum sealers
Avid Armor – www.avidarmor.com

ACKNOWLEDGMENTS

When I was approached with the opportunity to write this book, I was already a year into writing what I thought would become a small, self-published cookbook about venison. I saw the need for a book that helped people understand how make the most of every cut of venison. I had taken some amateur photos with a ring light in my in-laws' kitchen and was diligently perfecting my recipes when things took a welcomed turn into something bigger. I have more than a few people to thank for that.

To Thom O'Hearn, for your patience with me as a busy, scatter-brained, first-time writer. This book grew legs and took flight thanks to your guidance.

To Regina Grenier, Catrine Kelty, and Zack Bowen, for bringing my recipes to life and capturing them with such beauty. Your incredible work elevated this book into something greater than I could have imagined.

To Danielle, for being the most supportive sister. Whether I'm feeling overwhelmed, uncertain, or elated, I've turned to you for advice on every major event in my life. You've always led me in the right direction.

To Mom and Dad, for supporting me and encouraging me to chase my dreams. You've always made me feel loved. Thank you for giving us (Danielle, Jimmy, Tommy, and I) the foundation to grow into who we are today.

To Leslie and Michael, for believing in us. Your generosity and support have allowed us to create the life we always wanted. I'm forever grateful and appreciate you both.

To Nick, my husband and best friend. Words can't describe how much you mean to me. Thank you for giving me the confidence to do anything I set my mind to. I'm so proud of the life we've built together.

To my followers, for showing your appreciation. I'm touched by your messages and stories of new hunters finding their way, butchering their first deer, and learning how to cook. We've grown and learned a lot together.

To mother nature. It's cheesy, but I need to acknowledge how much the outdoors have done for me and my journey with food. My introduction to hunting was the catalyst into my desire to learn how to butcher and cook. Without your wild beauty, I may have never found my way.

ABOUT THE AUTHOR

Allie was born in Pittsburgh, Pennsylvania, and was drawn to the outdoors as a young girl. She grew up horseback riding, camping, and fishing with her family, and playing sports. During her college years at the University of Pittsburgh, she discovered hunting through her then boyfriend, now husband, Nick. She started documenting and sharing her outdoor adventures on social media in 2015 through "Outdoors Allie" as a way to connect with like-minded folks: those who hunt for their food, care deeply for wildlife and public land conservation, and enjoy sharing a cold one around a campfire. Her go-to cocktail is a spicy margarita from scratch and her guilty pleasure is eating raw cookie dough. As a kid, she swore she'd have a dog of her own and now she can proudly say she does.

INDEX